Patrick Darfler-Sweeney is someone I have known since my sophomore year in high school. He was not only my homeroom teacher and coach but also a mentor who I wanted to emulate. If you read *Fostering Parent Engagement for Equitable and Successful Schools* closely you will know why I felt that way about him many years ago and still do to this day. Too often we want to blame parents for not wanting to show up for their children, but Darfler-Sweeney wants to understand the family perspective, develop partnerships, and find ways to work together to have an impact on student learning, and he offers that guidance and practical steps in this very important and timely book.

Peter DeWitt, *Ed.D. CEO and Founder, Instructional Leadership Collective, USA*

Fostering Parent Engagement for Equitable and Successful Schools should be the reference guide for all school leaders who seek to create equitable opportunities for all their students. Common sense tells us that fully supportive families passionate about their children's academic success are critical to the results of any school.

Any education leader understands the wide variance in how families support their children in school. While Dr. Darfler-Sweeney's book addresses all families with a systemic approach to practical activities from prenatal to graduation, one group is often absent from traditional activities that attempt to inform parents about their child's progress. This group comprises parents who did not do well in school themselves and feel "school traumatized." They are too often judged not to fully care about supporting their children's progress. This book places them as a critical partner who should be supported on their terms and made to feel fully welcome.

For educators committed to providing an equitable opportunity for all students, Dr. Darfler-Sweeney's book will be the guide to empowering every family. We owe it to the success of our students to engage their families as a critical, constructive partner in learning. We finally have the resource guide many have been waiting for to support families and take a leap toward equity. I know that once this book is in your collection, you will turn to it repeatedly as a guide for family engagement.

Alan November, *Senior Partner at November Learning, USA*

Fostering Parent Engagement for Equitable and Successful Schools

Fostering Parent Engagement for Equitable and Successful Schools acknowledges and unpacks what educators have known for a long time: parents are the primary teachers of their children. This engaging book explores how schools can improve their relationship with parents and caregivers to develop a more equitable educational environment for all students. Designed for district and school leaders, this practical book helps readers apply the many leadership lessons taught in training programs and education leadership courses to improve their parent engagement as a function of effective education and not compliance. Full of real-world examples, reflection questions, "Actionable Ideas" checkpoints, and additional resources, this valuable resource encourages reflection while challenging leaders to improve and leverage parent and caregiver involvement in their children's education.

Patrick Darfler-Sweeney is a retired Superintendent of Schools of the Hunter-Tannersville CSD, New York, and is currently an Educational Consultant.

Other Eye On Education Books Available from Routledge
(www.routledge.com/eyeoneducation)

Finding Your Path as a Woman in School Leadership: A Guide for Educators, Allies, and Advocates
Kim Cofino and Christina Botbyl

Leading School Culture through Teacher Voice and Agency
Sally J. Zepeda, Philip D. Lanoue, David R. Shafer, and Grant M. Rivera

Becoming an International School Educator: Stories, Tips, and Insights from Teachers and Leaders
Edited by Dana Specker Watts and Jayson W. Richardson

The Principal's Desk Reference to Professional Standards: Actionable Strategies for Your Practice
Robyn Conrad Hansen and Frank D. Davidson

Trailblazers for Whole School Sustainability: Case Studies of Educators in Action
Cynthia L. Merse, Jennifer Seydel, Lisa A.W. Kensler, and David Sobel

Get Organized Digitally!: The Educator's Guide to Time Management
Frank Buck

The Confident School Leader: 7 Keys to Influence and Implement Change
Kara Knight

Empowering Teacher Leadership: Strategies and Systems to Realize Your School's Potential
Jeremy D. Visone

Fostering Parent Engagement for Equitable and Successful Schools

A Leader's Guide to Supporting Families and Students

Patrick Darfler-Sweeney

Routledge
Taylor & Francis Group
NEW YORK AND LONDON

Designed cover images: © Getty Images

First published 2025
by Routledge
605 Third Avenue, New York, NY 10158

and by Routledge
4 Park Square, Milton Park, Abingdon, Oxon, OX14 4RN

Routledge is an imprint of the Taylor & Francis Group, an informa business

© 2025 Patrick Darfler-Sweeney

The right of Patrick Darfler-Sweeney to be identified as author of this work has been asserted in accordance with sections 77 and 78 of the Copyright, Designs and Patents Act 1988.

All rights reserved. The purchase of this copyright material confers the right on the purchasing institution to photocopy or download pages which bear the support material icon and copyright line at the bottom of the page. No other parts of this book may be reprinted or reproduced or utilised in any form or by any electronic, mechanical, or other means, now known or hereafter invented, including photocopying and recording, or in any information storage or retrieval system, without permission in writing from the publishers.

Trademark notice: Product or corporate names may be trademarks or registered trademarks, and are used only for identification and explanation without intent to infringe.

ISBN: 9781032730387 (hbk)
ISBN: 9781032730370 (pbk)
ISBN: 9781003463399 (ebk)

DOI: 10.4324/9781003463399

Typeset in Palatino
by codeMantra

Access the Support Material: www.routledge.com/9781032730370

Dr. Earle Flatt, Siena College
Alan November, Seton Hall University and November Learning
        -Thank you for the guidance and inspiration for my education journey

Contents

Meet the Author xii
Foreword xiii
Preface xvii
Acknowledgments xix
Online Supplemental Resources xxi

1 Why 1
   Evolution 1
   What We Have Known for a Long Time 3
   Where It Started for Me 4
   Reflection 8
   Additional Resource 8

2 My Story 9
   The Power of Reality 9
   Reflection 12
   Additional Resources 12

3 A Matter of Equity 13
   eq·ui·ty /ˈekwədē/." 13
   Parent Involvement v. Parent Engagement 13
   Absenteeism 15
   Home Work: The Great Savior or the Devious Gap
      Enhancer? 16
   Digital Divide(d) 17
   Teacher-Parent Contact 21
   Logistical Constraints on Parents' Time in the "18" Zone 22
   We Pay You to Teach Our Kids 23
   Recognize That Their Child Is the Parent's Best Effort 25
   Actionable Ideas 25

Reflection 30
Additional Resources 30
References 31

4 Educating the Parents 32
Building Roads 32
Baby Steps 39
Supporting the Investment 43
Actionable Ideas 52
Reflection 60
Additional Resources 60
References 60

5 Creating Opportunities 61
The Traditional View 61
Extracurricular 62
Ideas for Programming 65
Actionable Ideas 66
Reflection 79
Additional Resources 79
References 79

6 Teacher-Administrator-School Community Leadership ... 80
Accepting the Need: Defining the Equity Issue for
   Everyone 80
A Thoughtful Balance between Information/
   Advocacy/Guiding/Opportunities 81
Honoring the "C": Call, Contact, Coordination,
   Collaboration (Denise 1999) 84
Just Focusing on the Student Without the Parent
   Connection Is Just Short-Sighted and Selfish 85
Revisit the Child Study Team 86
How to Employ Situational Leadership
   to Manage Your Vision 87
Actionable Ideas 89
Reflection 94
References 94

7 The Lesson of the Pandemic Digital Equity 95
A Crisis Is the Mother of Reform 95
My First Trip to the School Library 96
Actionable Ideas 101
Reflection 105
Additional Resources 106
References 106

8 The Good Stuff 107
Interdependent Nature of Education 107
Feedback Loops and Resource Articles 114
PK-12 Digital Sample Curriculum-Students 116
Case Study: Who Should Be in PD/PL 117
PK-12 Digital Sample Competency-Based Skills for
  Parents in Supporting Their Students 127
Reflection 129
Additional Resources 129

9 Final Thoughts 131
Dreaming 131
Context: Going Backward to Go Forward 132
Parents: The Guardians of Dreams 133
Recognizing Our Situation and Doing Something 134
Equity Is Not a Destination—The Longer View 135
Giving Someone Stuff Doesn't Mean They
  Have a Clue How to Use It 136
Educate, It Is What We Do Best 137
College and Career Ready 138
Reflection 139
Additional Resources 140

Meet the Author

Patrick Darfler-Sweeney earned his doctorate in Education Leadership from Seton Hall University. From 2007 until his retirement in June 2016, Patrick Darfler-Sweeney was the Superintendent of Schools at the Hunter-Tannersville CSD in the Northern Catskill Mountains of New York. Hunter-Tannersville High School is a top high school in the USA (US News & Report, 2014 & 2015), ranked regionally as a top science school (2016). Patrick served 18 years as a classroom teacher and athletics coach and 22 years as an administrator, principal, dean of students, athletic director, special education director, and superintendent. Professionally, he served on the NYSCOSS Commissioner's Advisory Council and legislative committees. Recently, Patrick has worked for the New York State Education Department as an education specialist and previously with the University of the State of New York Regents Research Fund as a project manager for the New York State Education Department and as a lead evaluator of classroom teachers and professional development programs. Patrick lives in Tannersville, NY, with his wife (and educator) Laurie and their daughter Molly.

Foreword

When my dad asked me to write the forward for his book, I was honestly unsure why. I have no background in education and have never been a parent, either. I responded that I did not feel qualified, but I was deeply touched that he felt strongly that I could do a good job. After a moment, he explained that he wanted me to give my perspective on growing up and my feelings about school and learning. He said that getting a perspective from the kid's point of view is just as important as giving advice. Again, I was touched and appreciated he trusted me with such a task. My mind began racing with ideas and stories, and I had difficulty deciding on just one. At first, I wanted to tell our history with cross country because every runner knows how deeply connected running is to everything. Instead, I decided on not just one snippet of time but rather the feelings behind them.

At a very young age, I remembered my parents encouraging me to learn, giving me room to figure things out, and making it seem as if it was better than chocolate. My parent's enthusiasm for education and the beauty of learning new things made me curious to know and do more. I was reading recently in the Harvard Journal that a person's intelligence is not something we are necessarily born with (though genetics do play some role). The most significant factor in our ability to retain knowledge comes from cultivating a positive learning environment at a young age with a "growth mindset."

I picked up on the emotions and attitudes of the adult figures in my life. I didn't fully understand concepts, but I understood the feeling and would try to emulate it. My parents always projected a positive outlook on what school was and what it could offer. As a child, I just knew it was something I had to attend and a place where new experiences and information were explored. My parents were the ones to tell me I had to go, but it was how they framed it that made me want to go. I even volunteered to go to summer school! My mother used to tell me I have the privilege that other kids worldwide did not. My father would say I was learning a superpower, the power of knowledge. To a kid, that's pretty cool to think! My parents' relationship with my schooling was that learning was a tool and a power, one that, if wielded right, would lead me to a lifelong passion for learning.

My education has shown up in many forms outside the classroom. I needed to learn to understand the scenarios and world around me constantly. One of my favorite stories that my mother loves to tell is about when I was a toddler; I loved to test myself, my abilities, and my boundaries like many toddlers do. Instead of inhibiting my curiosity, my mom would let me explore—even when it scared her half to death, and she would be hovering from behind as I tried to scale the kitchen cabinets. Believe it or not, that is how half my love for education came to be. This story was the first to come to my mind because it exemplifies what my parents instilled in me. That exploration of the world around me is the first stepping stone of taking the knowledge I have and building on it, all while they are giving me the room to do so.

There are countless memories throughout my schooling where this has played out, whether when I was working on homework, joining an extracurricular, or curious about learning something on my own, such as the birds that took residence in our backyard. Suppose I didn't understand something on a homework assignment; rather than sitting defeated if neither my parents nor I could help with an answer, I learned to go to my resources. You might think, well, duh, that is what we are taught, but not everyone understands the value. My father taught me to rely on those resources and understand that not everyone does. Having the insight and curiosity to find an answer sets critical thinkers apart from the average. "Knowing how to find an answer is just as, if not more, valuable than having an answer" is what Dad would always say. In school, I was told to have explanations for my work, but I learned that the reason why is not just because we are proving our point, but rather knowing if we need an answer, we know how to find it. Curiosity is the foundation of knowledge. That is how I learned how to find resources to identify birds by calls and was able to connect them visually. My parents took the time to explain any question and either showed me or explained the steps I needed. Sometimes, that would require my dad to inquire further about what I was asking, which would frustrate me because I thought I was clear. My dad would say it is to help articulate my thoughts, which I didn't realize was so important until later in life. By reintroducing me to tools, I have learned in the classroom and reinforced my knowledge through using tools to succeed.

They have told me I can do whatever I want. "You can become an astronaut" was my mom's line. The basic idea was that I could do whatever I set my mind to as long as I put my mind to it and put in the work… As my dad calls it, I became a "serial lister," making plans and small steps toward what I wanted. There is a massive reward for overcoming obstacles you want to tackle for a greater purpose. I understood that challenging myself was part of working toward what I wanted. I have realized that not everyone is mentally challenged early on in life, which can lead to problems of unfamiliarity later on, especially since I don't know a single person who was not tested. Being able to cultivate our will to engage our minds and push the limits is what allows us to achieve bigger dreams. At least, that has been the case for me since my parents taught me, allowing me to grow. As a family of runners, our mantra has always been to trust the process (like trusting our training plan), and the rewards will follow.

Although challenges in childhood can make for great college application essays, I have realized there is a reason so many schools ask for those stories. It is seeing who has learned to handle a situation and react. Having something you must overcome is good, but at least for me, it has allowed me to know to push myself. In many ways, I have never been a natural at specific things I am passionate about. One of those is the career field I work in and have studied. As someone who works in publishing, it might be a shock to know that I refused to read until about nine or ten. Later on in life, my parents told me that they had beaten themselves up about it, blaming their parenting for my lack of wanting to read, putting me so far behind that I had to see the school specialist. It is their consistency, the fact that they never gave up on the chance to show me the magic a book can bring, and the support I got in school. Although the reward of challenging further in my education and now my career can be attributed to working through those goals as a young child, it was also a goal for my parents. They never gave up on their dream of teaching me skills so I could have the best chance to develop a good life. They taught me how to learn and enjoy the process while showing me that sticking with a goal and trusting your work process can lead to.

Molly Darfler-Sweeney, January 2024

Preface

Makeup of *Fostering Parent Engagement for Equitable and Successful Schools: A Leader's Guide to Supporting Families and Students*

The events of 2020–2021 have put into view our needs and hurdles as education leaders. The effects of the pandemic are uneven on our society, and its effects disproportionately affect our poor, undereducated, and minority populations. We struggle with our identity, needs, and responsibility for one another. This struggle will remain mostly unabated until we provide an equitable pathway to education. The one truth that has remained in our collective history is that education is a primary pathway to opportunity. We need equity in education to hope to advance in ways that spur creativity and collective competition. The meritocracy we purport is in stark contrast to the current plight of the undereducated (over-represented by black, brown, and limited English speakers) compared to the advantages of our educated, privileged class. We must do better. The recommendations and ideas contained within are based on my personal experiences and influenced by research.

The heart of *Fostering Parent Engagement for Equitable and Successful Schools: A Leader's Guide to Supporting Families and Students* is to level the education opportunity field by recognizing the pivotal role parents play as students' primary teachers and fostering a commitment and approach that educates parents so that their dreams for their student can come from a more informed and advantaged foundation. The average time students are in school is roughly 6 hours per day; for the remaining 18 hours, they are under the supervision of their parents. This is the core reality for all of our students. Those fortunate to have parents with economic advantages understand that supporting and creatively providing experiences of our world have provided opportunities in life that our economically disadvantaged families cannot.

This book is focused on the premise that parents are students' primary teachers, and the balance of responsibility measured in time is decidedly on the parents; it only makes sense that we cultivate and support our primary teachers to improve students' success in school.

The recommendations' structure and heart are based on a practitioner's view informed by research, years of observation, and practical trial and error. Chapter 1 explores the "why" for such a book and the long-held observations by many in the field. Description of the underlying dynamic of "6 and 18" and how it is more or less the influencer structure to a student's learning is introduced. Chapter 2 is the context of my upbringing and the filter through which I have observed the dynamics surrounding the power of parent engagement and its equity effects on students. Chapter 3 explores many of the more common challenges facing parents and students in school life. Chapter 4 is the heart of building a structure and systems to educate parents as their children's primary teachers. The chapter details a process and structure that can be used and modified to fit any school's needs and requirements. Chapter 5 shifts to looking specifically at extracurricular activities and ideas and how a school can use what it is already doing to enhance its purpose and return on efforts that look to coordinate ideas found in the previous chapter. Chapter 6 delves into the role administration, teachers, and community leaders can and should exercise to increase parent engagement and equity, specifically to zero in on the collaborative approach needed to expand buy-in by all parts of the school community. Chapter 7 treats the specific challenges of digital equity, especially in light of the most recent experiences during the height of the COVID-19 pandemic. Chapter 8 is gathering resources and organizing ideas found in Chapters 1–7. Chapter 9 is my final thoughts and reflections on the entire Parent Engagement and Equity dynamic and a general call to action.

Reflection questions and bibliography are provided at the end of each chapter. In Chapters 3–8, you will find additional "Actionable Ideas", resources, and web addresses to seek further investigation and tools for your school. Leadership rules for actions are also included to offer guidance and direction from a practitioner's lens.

Acknowledgments

Many people have inspired and humbled me with their love and support to reach this completion goal. To these people mentioned and those not mentioned, I am eternally grateful.

The first person to recognize is the person I cannot remember who it is; all I honestly remember is that it was a male teacher and the power of what he said to me transcended the personality who delivered the fateful statement. Truthfully, his words were not the words of a singular observation but the sage wisdom of the collection of educators who preceded me. "…all you need to remember is 6 & 18…" To my unnamed sage, thank you.

Peter DeWitt, a former student athlete that I coached and was his homeroom teacher, has, in his career, become my teacher and I, his student. Peter is a well-respected educator and author to whom I am deeply indebted for challenging me professionally and personally as a person and educator. His guidance and insights have informed many of my educational leadership and reform perspectives.

My parents were my first and most significant teachers. Their dedication to me and my sisters' education was a study in grit, faith, and the undeniable formula of manners, above all else, coupled with hard work, will get you everywhere. Thank you, mom and dad.

This book is dedicated to two of the most influential teachers I had at the start of my teacher preparation training and as a doctoral education leadership student. Dr. Earle Flatt, Siena College, and Alan November, Seton Hall University and November Learning.

Dr. Earle Flatt, Siena College, was the most enthusiastic and insightful educator I had ever encountered to that point in my life. I could not wait to begin teaching students after classes with Dr. Flatt; his kind yet steely manner set him apart. Dr. Flatt had a unique perspective both inside and outside the classroom. He wove his web of educating and guiding his students to take on the challenges of teaching as much more than a profession and to elevate it to a calling.

Alan November, Seton Hall University and November Learning, was one of my professors at Seton Hall during my doctoral studies. He is genuinely an educating disruptor. His passion and dedication to the premise that collective wisdom, when honored and shared in the desire for growth, is always more powerful than isolated singular pursuits gets me excited to the core. The impact of the work he has personally inspired me to advance since our days at Seton Hall University is integral to the experiences I continue to advocate for advancing teaching and learning while constantly attempting to transform education. Teaching and learning in the digital age have many responsibilities and incredible opportunities.

To all my former colleagues, professors, and teachers, thank you. Your commitment to seeking excellence in yourselves and your students is never recognized enough and, unfortunately, is unfairly criticized too often. Please take the advice my daughter Molly once gave in a persuasive essay she was assigned to write in 5th grade. She generally advised teachers and penned this beauty: "...you should buy yourselves flowers when you get paid and enjoy them..."

Finally, to my family at Routledge, working with Heather Jarrow and Sofia Cohen has been essential to keeping me on target; I appreciate your steady guidance and encouragement and eagerly look forward to new projects.

Online Supplemental Resources

Some of the resources in this book can be accessed online by visiting this book's product page on our website: www.routledge.com/9781032730370 (then follow the links indicating support material, which you can then download directly).

- Basic Engagement Program Elements
- Chart of Activities
- K-12 Digital Citizenship Competencies for New York State
- PK-12 Digital Sample Competency-Based Skills for Parents in Supporting Their Students

1
Why

Evolution

I am still determining when the change happened; I am trying to remember if it was subtle or sudden. Growing up and attending K-12 schooling and well into my first years as a teacher from 1966 to 1990, the foundation of public education was straightforward; it was about student opportunity. Students had a right to the opportunity of education that the state education department and the local districts defined. There was no guarantee beyond the opportunity. Famous court cases made that clarification very clear, such as Donohue V. Copiague CSD, 1977. Donohue graduated high school with only the ability to read at the 4th-grade level, and his family sued for educational malpractice. The courts found that no tort issue existed because he was afforded the opportunity of education; how he and, by extension, his family took advantage of that opportunity rested squarely on their shoulders, not on the school district. Even the landmark case of Brown v. The Board of Education, Topeka, Kansas, 1954 was built upon the belief that separate but not equal was about opportunity, not the guaranteed outcome.

Contrary to the popular myth that states and localities did not test students at this time, I vividly recall those Iowa State

Test bubbles we had to fill out! The results were viewed as individual accounting, not system accounting. If you did not perform where you thought you should, it was about your efforts and application to the challenging task, not the school district. Agree with that approach or not; it was the attitude of the time and the belief that rules and regulations were built upon. This kind of approach was in line with the "rugged individualism" belief that permeated both the conservative and by application of guaranteed opportunity, the progressive movements of the late 19th and 20th centuries.

The bombshell in the report A Nation at Risk, 1983, was a fantastic tool that changed a national conversation and perception of education in the United States even though it has been discredited as not based on research but more in line with popular rhetoric. Perception is more important than pure facts, and this was *before* Twitter, now X, and Facebook. This report gave everyone from the ultra-conservative right to the ultra-liberal left avenues to pursue their advantage. In essence, it became a free-for-all, and the ultimate price to be paid for this energy was by school teachers and administrators. We were hung out to dry as a professional education community, especially in the K-12 realm. The effects of this momentum are still reverberating 40-plus years later.

Currently, the shift is starting to come back to opportunity as our society, in general, struggles with social justice issues, racial inequality, institutional bias, and competing claims of what it means to have a safe school environment. These are all lag indicators resulting from actions, inactions, and filters individuals and organizations use to make decisions. The real work of affecting these lag indicators must start with an accounting of our current situation. Our situation is systematic, and its dynamic has remained unchanged in the last 100 years. On average, schools have the students for six hours per day, and someone else has the same students for 18 hours per day- Monday through Friday. 6 and 18 are the two most important numbers in the balance of equity in education. What we choose to do with this reality determines the effectiveness of a child's education and defines the real opportunities the child will have.

Although I have been thinking about 6 and 18 for the last 40+ years, the need for understanding and action is more important now than ever. I believe 2020 will be remembered as this generation's version of my generation's 1968. In 1968, the country exploded in open discussion of patriotism, civil rights, women's rights, black rights, immigrant rights (California migrant workers), Cold War, Space Race, Dixie 'Crats vs Establishment Democrats, Moral Majority, flat heads vs. long hairs, and social justice. Does any of this sound familiar?

As the explosion in 1968 put into view our needs and hurdles, so have 2020. Instead of the Vietnam War, we have the war on the Pandemic. The effects of the Vietnam War were uneven on our society, as has the Pandemic, disproportionately affecting our poor, undereducated, and minority populations. We continue to struggle as a society with our identity, needs, and sense of responsibility for one another. I believe this struggle will remain mostly unabated until we provide an equitable pathway to education. The one truth that has remained in our collective history is education is a primary pathway to opportunity. Absent equity in education, we cannot as a people hope to advance in ways that spur creativity and a collective competition that more resembles the ideal meritocracy we give lip service to than the current society of the undereducated (over-represented by black, brown, and limited English speakers) and educated privileged.

The original working title of this book was "The Power of 6 & 18." The dynamic of understanding the effects of the variable of time that environment that students live in and its ultimate effect on their education is key to improving dreams, opportunities, and outcomes for students.

What We Have Known for a Long Time

6 and 18 is the structure that defines the limitations of public schooling in the United States. 6 and 18 represent the average time we spend with students under our supervision in this nation; the balance of 18 hours is under the parent's supervision. The significant issues we deal with will never be satisfactorily

addressed unless we find effective ways to approach this structural limitation of our student's education. Equity is the force to closing the achievement gap, social justice issues, and authentic social community engagement. Most frustrating is that those in education know and understand the structural challenge, yet education reformers rarely approach the problem from a practitioner's perspective.

As I am writing, our state and nation are facing the coronavirus pandemic or COVID-19. Schools closed to help flatten the expected growth of the disease. School leaders faced many dilemmas, including continuing instruction at home and providing meals and forms of daycare to segments of our population. As we work through "reopening," there are new challenges and the tendency to look back at what we have done in the past as ideal. Competent leadership has never been as premium as it is now. Hopefully, out of this, we will be able to reflect on what we need to work on to bring equity to all of the communities we serve. Unfortunately, as we are currently constructed, it becomes more apparent that the gap between equity and social mobility for our students will only be amplified. Even at this early juncture, it is evident that our economy will be severely hampered for an undetermined amount of time. Those with the best preparation and networks will better navigate the rough waters ahead than most. We are the individuals who must now, more than ever, advocate for structural changes that do not merely increase the accountability of the teachers and administrators but are guided by our teachers and administrators. We have to evolve our relationships with those who most directly determine the success of our students: the parents. We must *educate* our parents on how to be effective parents for their students to achieve the equity that we all seem to agree must happen.

Where It Started for Me

The year was 1983 when I started my teaching career, and a veteran teacher approached me and said, "Sweeney, let me tell you that there are only two things you need to remember 6 and 18."

He just walked away. I was dumbfounded because he seemed so sure of himself and stated with such solemness that I felt a little dumb for not getting what in blazes he was talking about. At first, the advice also struck me as only being marginally better than the typical banter I was getting from my experienced colleagues. They were in synch, telling me that I could now throw out all of that "useless" theory I was taught in college about teaching. What an endorsement for teaching preparation programs! I wish I could credit the teacher who gave me the 6 and 18 advice, but I honestly do not remember who it was. As time went on, his words haunt me to this day. I not only listened to his words, I felt them.

I taught history (social studies), coached three seasons every year: XC, XC Skiing/Bowling, Track and Field, chaperoned dances, trips, and clubs, and grew close to my brother and sister teachers, all understood the need to tip the 6 and 18 balance. When I became a school administrator, I supported and attended everything possible. I further understood that it had to be more than just showing up to be seen; I often stopped students in the hallways and classrooms to speak with them to let them know that I was there to see them and not for them to see me. They need to know I am proud of them and their choices.

We have examples of many students performing exceptionally well in our current system. 6 and 18 represent the average time we spend with students under our supervision in this nation; the balance of 18 hours is under the parent's supervision—Twenty-five percent of the day in school and 75% out of school. On weekends and the 12 weeks of the year of vacations and breaks, it is 0% in school. Compounding the equations with snow days, emergency days, school suspensions for discipline reasons, and sick days limits school contact time. Again, we know all of this, and the answer often proclaimed is, "well, our school calendar is an agrarian-based one that is not designed with today in mind- we need to go to school longer." There is nothing to support this thinking except one exception, which I will discuss later.

Children of parents who see education as an opportunity for their child to advance, learn, and ultimately flourish in life will likely do just fine in school. They are not their child's "best friend," nor the "super advocate" that comes rushing into the school to take down the teachers and administrators to show them their apparent ineptitude concerning their child. They are the parents who do not see the school as the enemy but rather as the necessary vehicle that will help them support their child's goal of having a better quality of life than they had. These parents partner with the school. They model the more significant lessons of skills for success in school and life so that their child is enveloped in the way of living. This seamless process has a clear path of opportunity as something that is developed and nurtured and not some gift of compliance, "I worked hard and kept my mouth shut, and THIS is what I get?"

Doesn't every parent want what is best for their child? Doesn't every parent support their child's well-being? Aren't all children the result of their parents' best efforts? The answer to all of these questions is mostly "yes." However, many parents do not know HOW to parent these outcomes for their children. We, as educators, know that we have talked about this dilemma many times in the hallways, faculty rooms, meetings, and post-observations. We suffer from institutionalized myopia in dealing with parents.

If you read many articles and testimonials of well-meaning educators and administrators, they love to talk about their amazing programs of reaching out to parents and their collaboration. Upon further review, I found that many of these measures of these well-meaning programs are no more than high-powered bulletin boards of information and broadcasting. Parents, who likely would already volunteer, work with the school. Those programs advance parents who have already engaged, not those who need involvement. By extension, the children of these parents who already "get it" are further advantaged.

Suppose we want to affect the 6 and 18 structure; we need to educate the parents on how to be parents of a student. Unless they are educators, parents only know their student's experiences; they only know and understand how to parent effective students if it was modeled for them as a child-student. This is the heart of the achievement gap that crosses all ethnicities, races, and socio-economic lives. It has no inherent bias and has a devastating and lasting effect.

The ever-growing concern of a divided opportunity for our minority, poor, and rural students continues to dominate our collective angst regarding what we need to do. In 2015, the National Policy Board for Educational Administration published its new standards called PSEL (Professional Standards for Educational Leaders), which replaced the previous standards known as the ISLLC Standards. The PSEL Standards stand out in their emphasis on equity, institutional bias, social justice, and community & parent outreach emphasis. These new dimensions of focus reflect the growing concerns both practitioners and researchers have concerning addressing the needs of our students. Further support of the PSEL Standards came in 2018 when the National Policy Board of Educational Administration published its National Educational Leadership Preparation Program Standards (NELP) for Building Level. The NELP standards for establishing a practice for preparation programs align with the PSEL Standards and add, reflecting the growing divide of equity, digital literacy, and citizenship across the board on the school building level.

I do not have all of the answers. I have some powerful experiences and ideas to guide a new approach. Many of the ideas are not new, but applying the concepts to a structured approach can, I believe, lead us to much more effective use of our time for our students' sake. We need to recognize that as the educational institutions of our children, we must have a parent curriculum to teach parents and provide the resources they need to be parents of students. Parents need to understand their responsibility in this social compact of public education and the impact of their actions on their children so that they make informed choices and decisions for their children. To summarize, we as educators protect our children's parental dreams; the better we can dream effectively, the better we can do our job.

> **Reflection**
>
> 1 If you could list at least three things you want parents to support with their student, what would it be, and why did you choose this idea?
> 2 Describe your ideal parent of a student (Note: this does not have to be an actual person).

Additional Resource

Darfler-Sweeney, P. J. (2010). *A cross sectional exploratory study of the New York State global history/geography regents*, 2001–2007. Seton Hall University.

2

My Story

The Power of Reality

I am the child of immigrants and school dropouts. My mother dropped out of school at 13, and my father dropped out at 16. After meeting in New York City, each earned their Graduation Equivalency Diplomas. According to standard measurements of risk factors, children of immigrants who dropped out of school and earned a G.E.D. are likely to be high school dropouts. Instead, my parents had three children who earned college degrees (all three), Professional Advanced Certificates/Licenses (all three), and a doctoral degree. How did this happen?

My parents were motivated by frustration and embarrassment of their inability to access opportunities for those with formal education and the just as crucial informal relationship education that happens concurrently in our schooling system. Without the burden of dropping out of school in our system, they concentrated on the reality that unfolded before them. To achieve their goal for their children—to have a better quality of life and better opportunities, their children needed to be educated. Whatever the school did or teachers requested, we were to do, no questions; they believed that because education was what we needed and the school was the vehicle we needed, the school was in charge; they were not our servants to provide us what we needed. In second grade, my teacher pulled me from the classroom to speak with her and another teacher about my pronunciation of the number "thirty." People who grew up in Ireland pronounce the "th" sound like a soft "t" sound rather than the US pronunciation as a hard "th" sound. The teachers told me that pronouncing the word thirty as "tirthy" was something that only ignorant people did, and I would start immediately pronouncing it correctly. I did what they told me, but I had no idea what an "ignorant" person was, and it did not sound good. When I got home and told my parents what happened, they quickly told me to learn how to pronounce it correctly as the teachers directed. That was the end; there were no outward demonstrations of outrage or immediate parent-teacher meetings to set them straight. No, it was simple; if their children were to succeed, we had to conform and learn in my parents' eyes. My parents put my education needs before their feelings; do not get me wrong, I believe the teachers were wrong in their approach and what they said; though I think they were doing it with the best intentions. Context is essential in understanding the powerful lesson my parents taught me that day.

How did my parents, who did not have the academic or even the school cultural knowledge and background, pull this off? In part, they benefited from not experiencing our system and getting caught up in emotions and experiences that affected them. They focused on basic skills that they did understand are needed for success in life. Devastated by the economic blockade of their country during World War II and the destruction of its European neighbors, Ireland was forced to forge its path. Many emigrated from the third-world economic conditions and sought a new start in the United States. In making a new life for themselves, they had to work, find jobs, keep those jobs, and make the most of what they could from the opportunities available. Without an education, high-paying jobs were not an option. The most they could do was rely on their relationships and networks to find employment and work hard. My parents believed that commitment, manners, working hard, learning your craft, and improving your skills would lead to advancement. These skills were foundational. If they could model and teach their children those same skills, the logic follows their children would advance in school—which was *our* job.

The children who often frustrate us as educators are a product of parents who have either not thought about their role in their child's schooling or simply have no idea how to parent a child in school. As educators, this situation isolates us from parents who are reluctant to engage and remain frustrated that they do not understand how to assist. I have countless examples speaking with teachers of middle and high school grades who refused to call and contact parents because they thought it should be up to the students to "take responsibility" for their actions; yet, as a matter of policy and practice, we do not have a structure that allows these very same students responsibilities to make choices about their futures! Try this test; look at the sheer number of rules of behavior of elementary school students versus the number of behavioral rules for middle and high school students. You will find that elementary students have far fewer behavioral rules! Yet we, educators, claim they should have more responsibilities with choices. Weird. The second effect of this isolation from parents is the attitude that their child's education is something they farm out to the schools to take care of, and they are off the hook; educators have become the parents' servants. A parent told me, "I work for her since she pays my salary." I told her I did not work for her, but for the students and the community and the state, but not her individually. I am unsure if she understood the meaning. Unfortunately, we have created this situation. We recognize that parents do not understand their role as their child's primary teacher; we have reacted to this situation via de facto isolation as to what we do, why we do it, and what the connection is between what we do and what they can be doing to maximize our collective efforts. Parents have developed this joint conclusion that schooling is an isolated activity that they pay taxes to be taken care of; the parents and students are the consumers, and we are the servers. Customers upset at the service complain they are not getting the expected value.

Many schools and districts have embarked on glorified information center programs. The underlying belief hope is that the parents will make better choices with more information. The problem is that if parents do not know that a real connection between what they do affects their child's success in school directly, it becomes confusing and further isolating—a significant unintended outcome.

The idea of a parents' curriculum is based on the premise that parents are the child's primary teachers with the most contact time. The essential skills for success in schools are taught and modeled at home, developed further in the schooling process, reflected upon at home, and reinforced at home and school. No person can know what they do not know. We are in the business of educating; educating is what we must do.

Reflection

1. Explain the relationship your parents had about your schooling.
2. What are your lasting memories of your parents and school? Why do you believe these memories came to your mind first?
3. Choose a life lesson taught by your parents that has been the most impactful in determining the person you are today.

Additional Resources

Picot, G., & Hou, F. (2011). Preparing for success in Canada and the United States: The determinants of educational attainment among the children of immigrants. *Statistics Canada Analytical Branch Studies Working Paper*, Catalogue no. 11F0019M — No. 332, ISSN 1205-9153, ISBN 9781100177472, pp. 1–28.

Shiffman, C. D. (2017). "It helps me to help them": A case study of parents in GED classrooms and their children. *Journal of Research and Practice for Adult Literacy, Secondary, and Basic Education*, 6(3), 5–18.

3
A Matter of Equity

eq·ui·ty / ˈekwədē/."

In education, the term equity refers to the principle of fairness. Fairness is as subjective a standard as anyone can find; it comes down to who judges the standard.

Soon, many questions arise: How many resources are committed to equity? And to what point does the pursuit of equity become an end unto itself? Often, problems that philosophically follow this path of reasoning become the dominating tension point rather than the simple proposition of whether or not a person or group of people can take advantage of equal opportunities.

Parent Involvement v. Parent Engagement

The ramifications for 6 and 18 define the standard's desired outcome to increase parent interaction:

> A school striving for family involvement often leads with its mouth—identifying projects, needs, and goals and then telling parents how they can contribute. A school

> striving for parent engagement, on the other hand, tends to lead with its ears—listening to what parents think, dream, and worry about.
>
> (Ferlazzo 2011)

In simple terms, parent involvement actions are those of compliance, while parental engagement is the action of education.

The compliance of parental involvement for some schools is all that they need. If the school serves economically well-off families, then the school's mission is to extend the already existing opportunities the families provide. Education costs can be more concentrated on academic and enhancing extracurricular supports and less on equity supports. Case in point, the district I retired from is considered as wealthy (two times the average wealth of a school district) as those in the wealthy suburban districts of the city. Our community has many second homeowners; thus, the formula includes their wealth. Our students have a free and reduced lunch rate of over 60%. Therefore, we receive the same state aid as these wealthy districts. My district uses the aid to pay for the basic operating needs of the district; our suburban counterparts can use the same assistance to enhance programming opportunities, pay their teachers more in salary, and provide a very different experience than we can.

The dynamic means we must understand what we know about student success as it relates to the actions of their parents and plan a course of education for parents. Then, parents could gain an understanding and have access to resources. These actions will serve as their equity vehicle for equal opportunity for their children. "The best predictor of student success is the extent to which families encourage learning at home and involve themselves in their child's education" (PTA 2000). Understanding the variables that make this a reality is something other than rocket science. Families face other more insidious challenges in their effect on students' ultimate school success. To better understand the most common factors driving inequity in the 6 and 18 balance, I picked a few of what I believe are the most representative challenges in most of our schools today.

Absenteeism

Absenteeism has become the focal point of many in the field as a situation that screams obvious and easy for most to understand why it directly connects to a student succeeding in school. Children chronically absent from school—meaning they miss more than 10% of the days—are much more likely to face educational challenges and become truant or drop out (Chang and Romero 2008; Gottfried 2011). The Research Report produced by the Urban Institute (https://www.urban.org/sites/default/files/publication/39151/2000083-insights-into-absenteeism-in-dcps-early-childhood-program.pdf) does a fantastic job of presenting the student chronic absenteeism issue in the intricate and tangled web of reasons for its causes and devastating effects. Chronic absenteeism starts as early as Pre-Kindergarten and is also the most critical time for an intervention. The District of Columbia Public Schools (DCPS) and its Early Childhood Education Division (ECED) studied its Head Start PK programs and the issue of absenteeism. They identified a few child and family factors that contributed to absenteeism. These factors included the family's relative prioritization of prekindergarten, logistical issues, personal challenges and significant family barriers, and parents' relationships with staff, schools, or teachers. In deconstructing these factors, it is easy to see that half of the primary reasons can be affected by the school's actions, and the remaining two can be affected by inter-community-municipal-school collaboration. This is a formal way to say the cooperating team.

Notice the word "prioritization" in addressing the importance of PK; many see this early grade as nothing more than a more formalized babysitting situation. Those in Early Childhood Education will argue that it is the foundational setting to set a student on the path to sustained success in school. As a result, many of our minority and low-income families, feeling uncomfortable with the school teachers and staff or demonstrating a lack of cultural awareness, will not ask for help. When we approach them, will they see it as an unwelcoming gesture or action unless we think it through systematically, with a tremendous amount of thought, conversation, and purpose to guide our actions.

Absenteeism is a lag indicator of the parents' situation and not in a silo as the lead indicator of student struggles academically. Fixing the latter without addressing the former is a sure way to lead to nothing. At many students' homes, the priorities are relatively consistent: a roof over their heads, food on the table, clothes to wear, and hope that tomorrow will be better. The relative means a family has—wealth, parental education, and social mobility (determined by their profession and, in many cases, skin color)—will dictate the ability of parents to prioritize their children's education. Supervision, physical space, and simple conversation about learning (curiosity) are left behind to satisfy the basic needs first.

Prioritizing education is necessary for a child's success in school, but it is far from the only variable. Some families can prioritize education, but if the logistical support of a stable home life (emotional and/or physical) is not present, the effectiveness of the idea of prioritization will not bear fruit. Too often, and this is not limited to schools, we seek immediate "fixes" for situations without examining first the context and structures that underlie the condition. It requires a systematic evaluation conducted first, identifying and analyzing the variables involved in starting a framework and approach that will constantly reevaluate its effect, needs, and changing requirements. In the words of an old Nike advertisement, "there is no finish line."

Home Work: The Great Savior or the Devious Gap Enhancer?

If you want to start a passionate argument among teachers debating the merits of assigning homework to students, be sure your health insurance is current and the coverage is comprehensive. In his literature review work *Visible Learning: A Synthesis of over 800 Meta-Analyses Related to Achievement* (2008), John Hattie concluded that current practice for homework on the primary level has zero effect on achievement, while in the secondary setting, it could have a positive impact on achievement.

Some in the field use this conclusion to support the idea that it is better not to assign homework since it will not provide a positive achievement effect in testing. Hattie points out how the construction of the homework assignment directly correlates to the achievement effect. In other words, most teachers and schools do not create their primary-aged homework assignments in a way that best improves student achievement. So, if teachers and a school wish to avoid gaining an advantage for their students through improving homework construction, they are better off not being negatively assigned. The key to understanding the conclusion drawn by Hattie is recognizing that many types of assignments are given to students and that the effect these assignments have on achievement will vary. For example, "…younger students can't undertake unsupported study as well, they can't filter out irrelevant information or avoid environmental distractions – and if they struggle, the overall effect can be negative." (Hattie 2008) Understanding this, it becomes clear that a student with a support system that can guide the process and control environmental distractions is at a distinct advantage over students whose families cannot provide this support. As a student enters high school, this support system is built upon and compounded over the years. The result is that while positive, measurable effects will vary, it most definitely could increase the achievement gap.

Digital Divide(d)

The current pandemic (COVID-19) has shed light on our readiness to use digital education to advance learning and teaching. It also has highlighted the gap between the haves and have-nots. In a bizarre way, the more underprepared our teachers are in facilitating world-class digital education, the less of an equity gap is present internally in the United States; however, the global gap is looming.

The issue has many layers: 1. Physical Tools: access to the internet and hardware (read: computers, tablets, laptops, smartphones); 2. Creating the $1,000 Pencil (November 2009)—dumbing down of digital technology—used to continue traditional forms of education and do not enhance the experience and may have the total opposite effect; and 3. Digital Education: facilitating lessons and environments that engage and connect students, teachers, and parents to collaborate and advance thoughts and ideas.

The easiest finding and enacting solutions are physical tools for the identified issues; still, access is only the first layer within this issue. Some schools and municipalities have or are in the process of creating this environment. It is essential to understand this is not an end unto itself. They may ignore it or use it as a paperweight if you build it. Affordability to connect to the internet and having a device to use are cost factors beyond just having the coverage of the digital world. Unfortunately, more needs to be done to assist with the cost of internet access, and the burden of the devices falls to families and schools whose budgets still need to be increased to support them. Interestingly, schools and digital access are considered "essential," but neither has seen enhanced funding…

Our experience across our country during the pandemic is the struggle of teacher and student engagement. Teachers need to understand the use of the digital environment. Students do not see the point of engaging anymore and, more importantly, differently than they did when attending in-person instruction. Many teachers who did not understand the digital environment simply fell back to what they did in the classroom and set up a mid-20th-century classroom on the computer. And we wonder why the students' engagement was no different from when they had in-classroom lessons! This is how you turn your device into a $1,000 pencil. I saw a teacher's website where they assigned photos of textbook pages to students to complete work that was not "handed back" (given feedback) for days…the laptop, internet, and classroom site are glorified fax machines.

Most parents, students, and teachers are consumers of the digital world and often mistake this activity for using technology. Real education can only occur with discovery, failure, application, reflection, and articulation. Absent those experiences, we merely focus on compliance and maintaining the current status quo while the inequity occurs internally in the country and globally continues to accelerate. As educators, we are bound ethically, and I would argue morally, to remain updated to stem the issues of inequity, racism, and social justice.

A Central Office must develop a team of marines to fill its ranks of teachers, staff, and administrators. Highly trained, fully engaged, who understand and act independently to adapt and execute the world-class education system we demand (Darfler-Sweeney, Ed Week, 2018). This cannot be achieved if we only apply a growth mindset but do not make it part of our digital footprint. One of the most depressing research I have seen came out of Stanford University (https://ed.stanford.edu/news/stanford-researchers-find-students-have-trouble-judging-credibility-information-online). Education scholars say youth are duped by sponsored content and don't always recognize the political bias of social messages (Donald 2016). (Please note this was completed before the 2016 presidential election.) Adults did not perform much better, especially educators and our current system of education, "In every case and at every level, we were taken aback by students' lack of preparation," the researchers reported (Donald 2016). This is serious stuff. We are past the tipping point; many in this country have historically depended upon traditional news outlets for their information. For years, before he retired, Walter Cronkite (special note: for those of you born in the 1980s and beyond, he was the iconic news anchor for CBS Evening News 1962–1981) was voted among the most trusted persons in America. As the idea of an "internet influencer" and social media as "newsie outlets" becomes more prevalent with no corresponding responsibility to speak truth and accountability, individuals' abilities to critically consume and understand sources of information become paramount in thoughtful decision-making. "Let the buyer beware" takes on a far more onerous meaning.

The need for proper professional learning/development is critical; the educators I have interacted with are sick and tired of sales pitches for the latest Learning Platforms promising the sky with seemingly thousands of bells and whistles they must learn. The result often is that the faculty and staff feel overwhelmed and have no idea if the current "thing" fits their needs as educators. This must stop. Educators need to understand the internet's dynamic and how the ability to provide immediate feedback, collaborate, and research is, at its core, the improvement systems of learning engagement.

Referring back to the Stanford 2016 Study, the implications of our current internet consumption are an erosion of the future of our social, civil, political, and economic well-being. Any curricular building must include Digital Literacy that provides for critical internet consumption.

How does this play out in homes where the 18 hours of supervision rarely support digital education but instead have an increasing reliance on digital consumption minus any critical analysis? Especially in the growing age of hybrid and online learning environments, the transition to creating student researchers who own their learning, problem-solve, collaborate, and create new learning is essential. This is not easy work, but it is familiar work. When we think about the newest education digital frontier, it is the role of AI or Artificial Intelligence (example: ChatGPT). Students are using it, but it challenges our traditional approaches to teaching and learning and certainly calls into question the authentic product produced by students. Who has the best access to it, and how is this translated into the quandary of education equity?

While the jury is still out in determining some of the best applications of AI in our education system on how we will have students use it, teachers use it, and ultimately, how parents can leverage its possibilities in leveling a playing field for their children, we must continue to research, question and engage with all of our communities. As of this writing, the thoughts on AI in the classroom currently center on ideas such as having students defend their work (authenticity) as part of the complete activity. Another that I gravitate to is using it as a launching pad for increasing students' deductive reasoning skills. This is the Sherlock Holmes approach, calling upon the idea of the formula in solving cases, the deductive dead body approach. Presented with a conclusion, idea, or situation, it becomes a challenge for the students to ask the questions that need to be answered to understand why we got to these endpoints or conclusions. What do I need to know to learn to get to that endpoint? Even though the technology is new and, in some ways, challenging, it still comes down to teaching how to ask deeper and better questions for deeper and more comprehensive understandings.

When the purpose of professional learning/development is the driving force and not simply the use of a program or platform, the PL/PD has context and meaning familiar to any educator. Technology and the Digital Environment are merely the tools for the desired outcome, not the other way around. Once educators have a handle on both the context and applications of a digital footprint, then they can effectively facilitate for students and parents. Practical programs that use context and application as the foundation will succeed tremendously with students and parents.

Teacher-Parent Contact

One of the essential elements of student success is the support from parents in the 18-hour balance. "…that even after controlling for diverse socio-demographic variables (e.g., the educational and employment levels of both parents, child's grade, gender, and race), the strongest predictor of parent involvement was the parents' perceptions of teacher outreach. Specifically, the more parents perceived their child's teacher as valuing their contribution to their child's education, trying to keep them informed about their child's strengths and weaknesses, and providing them with specific suggestions to help their child, the higher the parents' involvement was both at home and school (Patrikakou and Weissberg 2000). How does this happen when many who are challenged by circumstance, culture, and race see schools, their teachers, and administrators as either unwilling or, worse, view schools as uncaring and repressive institutions?

Suppose schools want to affect positive change in the 18-hour balance. In that case, they must follow the same path as all learners—out of their failure (ineffective connection and engagement with parents), they must get immediate feedback and apply the new meaning to the improvement goal of educating themselves, parents, and guardians. It is a package deal; one without the other is doomed for failure.

At the beginning of the book, I talked about the simple advice I received as a doctoral student, "people don't know what they don't know." Applying this advice is for both our schools and the parents of our students. Schools need to come to grips with what parents and guardians understand and do not understand about raising a child for success in school. Schools need to understand why some parents and guardians do not feel connected to the school, nor do they believe they have any cultural understanding of their circumstances or appreciation of economic realities. The actual, effective intervention can be accomplished until these two sides of the same coin are understood.

Logistical Constraints on Parents' Time in the "18" Zone

Logistics is generally the detailed organization and implementation of a complex operation. The large organization for our purposes is the family unit—in whatever manner it is constructed. Understanding how a family provides necessities for its members is key to understanding a student's academic and social development foundation. The idea of the nuclear family consisting of a mother, father, and children, with one parent working to provide financial security and one parent at home as the primary child-rearing entity, has not been real in the United States since the 1960s. In fact, for those families who economically struggle, this includes an over-representation of black & brown families; it may never have been a "norm." The share of U.S. children living with an unmarried parent has more than doubled since 1968, jumping from 13% to 32% in 2017. That trend has been accompanied by a drop in the share of children living with two married parents, down from 85% in 1968 to 65%. Some 3% of children are not living with any parents, according to a new Pew Research Center analysis of U.S. Census Bureau data (https://rb.gy/uofvsq).

Given the structural makeup that is more of the norm for families, it is interesting to note the adjustments those families of means have made. While not having one adult at home as in the past, families now have more income but need more income to provide structured opportunities that deliver the experiences they want for their children. While at the same time paying for the supervision of their child. Meanwhile, children of families with fewer means have fewer options. Their priority is for the care of their children and not the opportunity because they cannot pay for it. Schools have attempted to provide extended day programs. Still, since the school is taking the initiative for such programs, parents need more input on the child's experiences and a grounding or understanding of what those experiences could or should be.

Conversely, families of means put a premium on holding their child's providers of structured experiences accountable for their programs since they are directly paying for those programs. And there lies the rub: families of means do not see it as their obligation to pay (in terms of taxes) for the opportunities of the less able and vote against and pressure school boards not to provide for others. The families of means do not see the collective value of all children having opportunities; most see it as creating an unfair system of those who have less gain more without paying or sacrificing for the opportunity.

The critical piece of extending the school day for families in need is to go further and educate the parents beyond the simple: we will babysit and supervise your children. This process of educating parents enables them to build on the opportunity at home and develop a mutual support structure in the child's education. Only then can parents become active partners in their children's educational opportunities.

We Pay You to Teach Our Kids

How often have you sat in parent-teacher conferences and heard, "I tell my daughter/son to do their work, but they don't listen to me"? For most, this is escape communication. After all, the parent has just relieved themselves of what they think is their responsibility, and how can you, as the teacher, possibly find fault? The parent has just handed over their role to you. An old friend and colleague once told me, "…you know we are only a meal and a bed from being an orphanage…" Why does this happen? If most parents want what is best for their children, why do these parents not engage with the school and its teachers? There are barriers, some obvious and others less so. England has a strict social structure; interestingly, one of the "jewels" of its former empire, India, has a caste system. This fact is taught in schools across the United States to emphasize the difference in our social strata. In truth, this romantic version of our social strata never existed. We continue to be divided by wealth, access to it, ethnicity, and race. "Others, like low-income or minority families, feel that staff (teachers and support staff) make them uncomfortable or show a lack of cultural awareness" (De La Torre 2016). It is clear to all involved the differences that each circumstance has. The great foundation of opportunity is in education, but it is NOT a solution to ethnic and racial bias; that is a much more complicated road to travel.

Parents who are low-income minorities or those who do not speak English are hyper-aware that teachers and school staff are not like them. The language we use, the clothes we wear, and the subtle ways we interact with one another are different and identify us. Success in school is dominated by those who are white, not financially poor, and speak English fluently.

Students of non-engaged parents with the school are more likely to have low self-esteem, need redirection in the classroom, and develop behavioral issues (Sheldon and Jung 2015); therefore, these students require extra services that cost more money. More impoverished children cost more money to educate. Schools can address symptoms of structural problems but never get to the root cause. To improve the circumstances of these students so that we can foster the equity they need, we need to educate the parents and service their needs as parent educators while at the same time addressing the immediate concerns that the students are presenting.

Educating parents about how to be parents of students and connecting them with resources is the most direct route to getting these students on the path of equity and informed choices of equal opportunity. Suppose we are serious about helping all our students and directing them to more community-building opportunities. In that case, we need to recognize the power that all parents of students have in the 6 and 18 balance.

Recognize That Their Child Is the Parent's Best Effort

If they did graduate, the parents, who were unsuccessful in school and struggled to graduate, do not see or hold their school experience in high regard. Many view schools as institutions that told them they were wrong, a failure, and not worthy of their time and resources. Rarely are these children told they have value, that their efforts were positive or good persons, and most importantly, that we care for them. For the most part, our system needs to be structurally set up that way. If the square peg cannot fit in our round hole, we either metaphorically beat it into the hole or simply give up and throw the piece away with a symbolic sigh. Understand this is a gross generalization, but many can identify that the perception of those who have failed in the system generally feels this way. Perception drives decision-making, not the vacuum of our intentions and actions.

When these children who have "failed" in our school have their children, psychologically, it is powerful. They did this thing right; they brought a child into this world—they did not "fail" in this task. This child represents that parent's best effort and pities anyone who challenges that truth in any way; this is how most parents of any background feel. That child is an extension of who they are; they will protect their child as they go to school. This may be fighting the school, defending the child blindly, or ignoring the school. Worse, the parent's negative attitude about the school generally reinforces 18 hours per day, 40 weeks per year. Unless there is careful and precise intervention on the part of schools and educators, this situation will not change.

 Actionable Ideas

School Equity Survey

Determining or getting an idea of the depth of self-examination your school or district needs to challenge itself is the logical first step to creating the space for collaboration and improvement. Using a school equity survey or inventory can provide the first step. To get a complete sense of what the school or district is facing, have representative groups from all sectors of the school community take and share their thoughts.

Equity in schools is one of the most debated but generally agreed-upon goals of many schools throughout the United States. The challenge is determining what type of equity is the goal. Is the equity we are seeking limited to the boundaries of Race? Gender? Ethnicity? Digital? Socio-economic status? Or is it encompassing all these "boundaries?" And how do we define "equity" in schools? Is it purely by offerings, or do we need to delve deeper into the opportunities and pathways to access and increase the chances of engagement and ultimate success? Getting a handle on this is essential to get everyone on the same page of understanding what the guiding idea and goals are to produce. The ideas and goals determine the purpose of action.

Once the action's purpose is determined, the following steps are to identify the current situation when examining perception and data. Illuminating the contextual background of information provides a fuller view of what a school is attempting to modify or improve. Too often, schools invoke actions and changes in vacuums of best practices that neither fit nor address the unique variables of the communities they serve.

Surveys and performance data can give a clearer picture of the current situation. It does not necessarily paint a complete picture, which is why all well-designed studies take great pains to illustrate the study's limitations. Testing results only give data about the questions tested. Causality is not assigned because too many factors can and often do play into a human performance outcome. Surveys are a collection of selected perceptions of situations. While surveys are also limited to the situations chosen, statements, and issues presented for responses, they offer or can offer a different view of a situation. Triangulating these data points may show a more complete picture of a situation.

A mistake I have seen many times in education is the misapplication of data and survey results, taking a lag indicator, the current situation, and simply assigning it a lead indicator action as the "cure." It is too simplistic to turn around a lag indicator and designate it as a lead indicator action. An absence of understanding of the variables and their interplay often leads to many unintended outcomes of the "reform."

Resource Connection: https://www.edutopia.org/article/beginning-year-equity-survey (Retrieved December 3, 2022)

Resource Connection: 34 Questions to Gather Feedback from Teachers and Staff on Equity and Inclusion: Equity Survey Questions

Parent Engagement

Scope: Parent engagement includes a holistic view of the parent's role in a child's education, extending beyond school-related events to encompass activities and interactions at home that contribute to a positive learning environment.

Sites:

68 Parent involvement Ideas that really Work—Georgia Department of Education:

https://www.gadoe.org/School-Improvement/Federal-Programs/Documents/Parent%20Involvement%20Ideas.pdf (Retrieved December 4, 2023).

Family engagement plan suggested activities—Texas Education Agency:

https://tea.texas.gov/academics/early-childhood-education/fe-plan-activities.pdf (Retrieved December 4, 2023).

10 Family Engagement Activities for Your Childcare Program—brightwheel blog:

https://mybrightwheel.com/blog/boost-family-participation-at-your-childcare-center-or-preschool (Retrieved December 4, 2023).

Article: historical perspective of the evolving views on parental engagement in school—Kappan:

https://kappanonline.org/evolving-views-parental-engagement-preston/ (Retrieved December 4, 2023).

Article: Improving how schools engage families during the crucial 9th grade year—Kappan

https://kappanonline.org/engage-families-9th-grade-mac-iver-epstein-sheldon/ (Retrieved December 4, 2023).

Absenteeism

Make education a family priority. Encourage your child to get more involved with their school. Sign them up for extra-curricular activities they like or an after-school program. Studies show the more involved a child and parents are with their school, the better their attendance and success is (Richmond County School System).

Sites:

10 High-yield actions to improve student attendance—NASSP: https://www.nassp.org/publication/principal-leadership/volume-17-2016-2017/principal-leadership-december-2016/10-high-yield-actions-to-improve-student-attendance/ (Retrieved December 4, 2023).

Best practices for improving attendance—Washington Office of Superintendent of Public Instruction:

https://ospi.k12.wa.us/student-success/support-programs/attendance-chronic-absenteeism-and-truancy/best-practices-improving-attendance (Retrieved December 4, 2023).

Homework

Site:

5 Ways to Get Parents Involved in Student Learning Beyond Homework—Getting Smart (Vlada Lotkina) (Retrieved December 4, 2023).

Engagement Plan Suggested Activities

AI/ChatGPT

Query: List ways AI can be used to close the education gap of economically disadvantaged students

ChatGPT Result:

AI has the potential to address educational disparities and close the education gap for students, especially those from economically disadvantaged backgrounds. Here are several ways AI can be utilized for this purpose:

Personalized Learning Platforms

AI-powered platforms can tailor educational content to individual students, adapting to their learning styles, pace, and preferences. This personalized approach can help students needing help with traditional teaching methods.

Tutoring and Homework Assistance:
AI-powered tutoring systems can support students outside the classroom, offering real-time help with homework, explaining concepts, and targeted assistance in areas where a student may be struggling.

Adaptive Assessments
AI can create adaptive assessments that adjust difficulty based on a student's performance, ensuring that each student is appropriately challenged and receives feedback to address their learning needs.

Language Learning Apps
For students who are English language learners, AI-driven language learning applications can offer customized lessons, pronunciation support, and interactive exercises to enhance language skills.

Early Intervention Systems
AI algorithms can identify early signs of academic challenges or learning disabilities, allowing educators to intervene proactively and provide tailored support to prevent long-term academic gaps.

Virtual Classrooms and Remote Learning
AI-powered virtual classrooms can enable students to access high-quality education remotely, reducing geographical and economic barriers. This is particularly relevant in situations where physical attendance may be challenging.

Digital Literacy Programs
AI can be utilized to enhance digital literacy skills, ensuring that students from all backgrounds have the necessary technological skills to succeed in the modern world.
Automated Grading and Feedback:
AI can automate routine grading tasks, allowing teachers to focus more on personalized feedback and instruction. This

efficiency can free up time for educators to provide additional support to struggling students.

Data Analytics for Decision-Making
AI analytics can help educators identify patterns and trends in student performance data, enabling data-informed decision-making to address specific challenges and implement targeted interventions.

Accessible Educational Content
AI can assist in creating accessible content, including text-to-speech features, subtitles, and other tools that cater to diverse learning needs, ensuring that no student is left behind due to accessibility issues.

Integrating these AI applications thoughtfully is essential, considering ethical considerations and ensuring that they complement, rather than replace, the valuable human element in education. Collaboration between educators, policymakers, and technology developers is crucial for successful implementation.

Reflection

1. If you could address any equity issue in your school, what would it be, why, and who, and what resources -aside from funding -would you need?
2. Choose and defend what you believe is the biggest equity challenge we face today in our pursuit to educate students.

Additional Resources

Alphin, Jr., H. C., Lavine, J., & Chan, R. Y. (Eds.). (2017). *Disability and equity in higher education accessibility*. IGI Global.

Dubay, L., & Holla, N. (2015). *Absenteeism in DC public schools early education program: An update for school year 2013–14*. Research Report. Urban Institute.

Ferlazzo, L., & Hammond, L. (2009). *Building parent engagement in schools*. Bloomsbury Publishing USA.

References

Chang, H. N., & Romero, M. (2008). *Present, engaged, and accounted for: The critical importance of addressing chronic absence in the early grades*. Report. National Center for Children in Poverty.

De La Torre, C. (2016). *Latino parent leadership: Through the eyes of Latino parent leaders*.

Donald, B. (2016). *Stanford researchers find students have trouble judging the credibility of information online*. News Center.

Ferlazzo, L. (2011). Involvement or engagement? Vol. 68. https://www.ascd.org/el/articles/involvement-or-engagement (Retrieved January 5, 2024).

Gottfried, M. A. (2011). The detrimental effects of missing school: Evidence from urban siblings. *American Journal of Education, 117*(2), 147–182.

Hattie, J. (2008). *Visible learning: A synthesis of over 800 meta-analyses relating to achievement*. Routledge.

Jung, S. B., & Sheldon, S. (2020). Connecting dimensions of school leadership for partnerships with school and teacher practices of family engagement. *School Community Journal, 30*(1), 9–32.

National PTA (US). (2000). *Building successful partnerships: A guide for developing parent and family involvement programs*. National Educational Service.

November, A. (Ed.). (2009). *Empowering students with technology*. Corwin Press.

Patrikakou, E. N., & Weissberg, R. P. (2000). Parents' perceptions of teacher outreach and parent involvement in children's education. *Journal of Prevention & Intervention in the Community, 20*(1–2), 103–119. https://doi.org/10.1300/J005v20n01_08

https://www.edweek.org/education/opinion-response-authoritarian-style-mandates-from-central-offices-dont-work/2018/07 (Retrieved December 3, 2023).

https://www.michigan.gov/-/media/Project/Websites/mde/educator_services/prof_practices/code_of_ethics.pdf?rev=017460345b4e44a2959f0558a3638d82. (Retrieved December 4, 2023).

4

Educating the Parents

Building Roads

They Don't Know What They Don't Know

I hope to have the opportunity again to address parents of toddlers at some point; I wish I had this idea when I started in education. I would be most enthusiastic and passionate about welcoming them and their children into the school community. Congratulations to them on their wonderful accomplishment of becoming parents and recognizing their most crucial role in our community as the primary teachers of their children. I would transition my story to being a parent and having the hopes, dreams, and aspirations we had for our daughter and assure them that their dreams for their child have the support of resources they can access. I would talk about the pathway of making their dreams for their child become their child's dream for themselves. I would commit the school to partner with the community and the parents. We will assist as their mentor as their child's teachers and help tailor the needs they will have to support the transition of the parent/guardian dreams into the reality of the child's dreams for themselves.

They don't know what they don't know. These words from my doctoral dissertation mentor changed my filter for understanding how I should approach all aspects of leadership. The concept of original thought is an illusion, as is objectivity. Humans can never achieve neutrality; it is impossible to account for each individual's endless combinations of experiences, genetic tools, and emotional development. It is possible to accept that we cannot expect anyone to act upon or understand what they do not know or understand; this is why no one can have a completely original thought—every new idea results from experiences, lessons learned, and modifying previous applications of thoughts and efforts. The lack of knowing something creates a vacuum of rationalization to come to an understanding of a situation. Early in my education as a historian, my professor asked what is more important in history, the facts or what we perceive as the truth. Facts do not drive decisions. The perception of reality drives the decisions and actions of individuals.

Many teachers and administrators are frustrated when public members speak as though they understand what it is to be an educator or administrator. Since everyone is required by law to attend school, homeschooling aside, the assumption is that everyone understands education. Those who attended school know the student experience, not the teacher or administrator experience. The public's experience as students and how their parents approached parenting informs how the parents of our students today interact with their child's education and the school.

The 6 and 18 reality of our education system is key to understanding the fundamental equity issues of our educational opportunities. Research indicates that less than 30% of student's academic success is attributable to schools and teachers. (Berliner and Glass 2014).The most significant variable is socioeconomic status, followed by the neighborhood, the psychological quality of the home environment, and the support of physical health provided (Berliner and Glass 2014). The socioeconomic status and neighborhood variables are the lag indications of education attainment and application, determining how powerful the education variable becomes. Leaving the "psychological quality of the home environment, and support of the health provided" as the primary lead indicators of a student's success. The parent or guardian is the student's home environment and health support provider. Therefore, the best effort is to educate the student's parents and put resources within reach of the home. This paradigm offers the best amplification of the effectiveness of the classroom teacher.

Cost is a factor, and too often, those who oppose better funding for education argue that money doesn't matter because the outcomes are unchanged. The research on this matter is clear. When school districts with sufficient resources are compared with those without, achievement outcomes are definitively higher in the wealthier districts (Berliner and Glass 2014). Students who live in poverty cost more to educate; their barriers to equal education opportunities demand extra services to be in the same relative position as their more affluent peers to take advantage of the same education system. If we are serious about equity in education, we need to ask better questions about the time, approach, and costs we are investing. Often, we are correctly trying to address the manifestations of the core issue—the lack of executive function, often leading to behavioral problems, disconnection, and loss of hope. Due to not connecting to the world, the educators are products of the educators who cannot connect to the students' world. The worst issue is not being motivated and disconnected from the vision of education other than a mandatory compliance nuisance. The core issue is their primary teacher in life, the parents or guardian. Suppose the primary teacher does not understand and accept that tremendous responsibility. In that case, the student is at a massive disadvantage, and their hope of taking advantage of education's immense array of opportunities is stunted. Schools must develop a curriculum for parents of students. It must begin as close to birth as possible.

Form Follows Function

A quote from W. Edwards Deming is spot on: "If you can't describe what you are doing as a process, you don't know what you're doing."

Research shows that the climate of an organization influences an individual's contribution far more than the individual himself.

A child's education is a process that is both basic in its structure and highly complicated in all variables that affect the child's engagement and outcome. Its structure is the heart of the 6 and 18 balance. A child's primary teacher is the parent, and the school becomes the primary institution of the social processing of academic distribution. In other words, what a child comes to the school building in terms of everything (physical, social, emotional, and prior-continuing learning experiences) is what the school will amplify over time. Rarely will a school alone overcome all the hurdles that prevent children from taking full advantage of the educational opportunities provided to them. Recognition of the parent's primary role and active engagement and education of the parent of a student is the logical path for improving the current inequities in educational opportunities that afflict the poor and minority (read: black and brown families) communities. The likelihood of success in the relationship between the school community and the parents must be targeted for improvement and growth with support, resources, and mentors to guide them in the journey. The key takeaway is the development of relationships that connect parents or guardians to the school community and the supportive services that make that connection easier to attain.

Needs Inventory

Two of the leading indicators of success in school are related to the home environment's psychological quality and physical health support. Many variables play into these conditions. Everything from what parents can provide as a result of their incomes to their own attitudes and importance of education, education curiosity, the positive fostering of curiosity, and means to provide meaningful contact time with students.

Schools have become the encompassing institution of societal development and their primary mission of academics. Many other municipal and community-based institutions and agencies have emerged over time to address their community members' actual and perceived needs. Some institutions and agencies directly result from legislation, while others are out of home-grown interest. Each of these groups has powerful and critical views and ideas of their family's situations and how to best assist in addressing the needs they see before them. To begin providing the best education for parents, it makes sense to pull these groups together and cull ideas. Secure commitments to collaborate on what parents need to know about raising students and recognizing that being a good parent means being a good parent of a student. Formulating a needs assessment of parenting is the vital first step as to what information and relationships need to be established to increase the likelihood of success. Schools, doctors, clinics, family services, community, and church organizations can provide information and contacts.

School leaders must assemble these groups and conduct ongoing authentic needs assessments of parents and guardians in their community. Once this needs assessment is developed, convert it to competencies that should be goals for effective parenting. Each competency should connect to information, education, resources (and how to get these resources), and contact information. This collaborative "Parent School Community Study Team" must meet and review progress, assess the current status of its families, and make all needed changes and adjustments at least every three months. This collaborative process needs to be ongoing and have a commitment by all partners to establish a doable reflection instrument based on observation and supported by data.

Build the Pipeline with the Community

I am not sure which cliche works best: "Necessity is the mother of invention," "If you build it, they will come," or perhaps, "Institutions transcend its people and purpose." Whichever one you most identify with will suffice. In our society, we have evolved several organizations and institutions to assist our neighbors in living, health, recreation, local economy, education, religious, ethnic, and political beliefs, to name a few. Each of these has a common structural element: they tend to operate in separate silos to concentrate on the singular purpose they were created to assist.

Understanding the silo mentality of these organizations and institutions is key to bringing them together in a coordinated exercise. For example, the school had established a cooperative agreement with a local hospital group for mental health counseling at one school. After retiring as a full-time school administrator, I was brought in as an interim. Great idea; however, the teachers and staff felt that important information needed to be heard, and the school was viewed as the problem rather than an avenue for student assistance. I asked for a meeting with the hospital group and attempted to open up a dialogue of the concerns to seek a workable solution. The meeting was not met with that "warm and fuzzy" feeling; we are in it together for the best of our students. Instead, I was confronted with a group determined to do what they felt was best and that we just needed to get out of the way and let me know that I was not the expert they were and to back off and leave them alone. I had hoped to work together without compromising confidentiality, specifically for their staff to suggest or even give us some in-service workshops on how we could approach our students to support their work. Unfortunately, this was met with dismissal on their part. Despite this experience, it leads me to an incredibly important lesson.

Established institutions rarely intend to adapt or change what they do to meet a partner's needs. Their attitude is often, "you came to me, we already have a great program we will gladly do what we are already doing but this time with you." Of course, there are exceptions to this very broad statement, much like the English language, where there is almost an exception to every rule. However, my experience is that schools and other institutions do not understand that BOTH sides of a partnership need to adapt to the specific needs of their new circumstance and not slap on what they are currently doing that fits a different (though similar) circumstance.

Well-thought-out leveraging points must be established beforehand so that the new partnership works adaptively toward the new circumstance, in this case, building a solid partnership foundation for parents as their child's primary teacher. The leveraging edge that schools have is that all children must, by law, go to school; therefore, access to the very families these groups, organizations, and institutions depend on is literally on our doorstep every day.

The key is the opportunity to build the relationship. The pipeline is filtered to connect the school and the families to the groups, organizations, and institutions that make it easier for the parents to function as their child's primary teacher and build on new dreams and opportunities for the next generation. If you think about it, who or what group could disagree with that as a foundational premise?

At the heart of the pipeline is understanding what the needs are of the parents and families and web together the different organizations, groups, and institutions that can provide and connect the vision as an interdependent entity that requires these "silos" to do what they do best in a coordinated fashion to maximize their efforts.

Setting the Stage: The Basics

Personal experiences inform many, if not all, of our choices. When I was doing a post-retirement interim position as an Assistant Superintendent/Principal, an elementary teacher lamented that she had completed a straw poll of her students to find out what they wanted to be when they grew up. Her concern was that all of the student's responses were aspiring to low-paying and minimally skilled positions. I asked her if she believed the students often traveled outside the community, and she said no. I then asked her if their parents often traveled to locations outside of our community; again, she didn't think so. Finally, based on the life they experience directly, are you surprised?

The story is not an indictment of jobs and professions and those that our society demands but rather the power of experience and curiosity in life. Our parents teach values and lessons corresponding to their children's knowledge and expertise. Many of our poor, minority, and limited English-speaking families are not prepared to create a pathway for their students that may extend beyond their current circumstances and experiences. They need our community education system to assist them so that our primary function of educating children is at its most effective.

Knowledge is power; learning about something is the first step in dreaming about something. Dreaming about something is the basis of making a goal. I remember, as a student and later as a teacher and administrator, the guidance counselors and teachers speaking to students and showing them the statistics of what students with no high school diploma versus having a professional trade certificate or license versus a college degree make for a living in terms of pay/salary. As a side note, this is usually done during high school, which for many is too late (perhaps a topic for another book) and seldom includes parents.

Parents can only request and act upon resources, ideas, and needs if they know what they are; this basis must be the foundation for developing a cooperative academic experience for their students. The counselors/mentors of the parents need to educate new parents and come to it by empowering them to get knowledge and bring them down the path of dreaming and goal setting for their students. Make this collaborative process of first engaging with the parents of the pathways open to their students and encourage the systems and structures that will ultimately improve the likelihood of these dreams.

Baby Steps

The Prenatal Network: Connecting the Ideas of Physical Needs, Social-Emotional Needs, How, Where to Connect

While I was administrator, our Elementary Principal, Melinda McCool, and I had an idea to develop and put together a type of "welcome to the world" basket for parents of newborns. The hope we shared was to provide new parents with a welcome letter to the district and a collection of helpful contact information (doctors, clinics, family service, community resources), pamphlets on child development, nutrition, reading, and number recognition. Melinda and her team did an outstanding job creating the basket and its early distribution. Still, we could not improve upon our idea due to other needs in the district and the realization that we needed personnel committed to this work more precisely.

We were on to something with this idea and effort. The premise is if we connect and nurture a relationship early with parents, we have a much better opportunity to cultivate a positive vibe and perception that the school is a team and that the parents and the child are members from the start. The reality is that after the child is born, the parent is the sole agent of education, socialization, and emotional connections. The school lurks as this ivory tower of rules and club norms that only members can engage in and use to their advantage. The more unsuccessful a parent was as a student, the more imposing and threatening this institution looms. The idea of the basket is to create a welcoming and partnering environment from the very start. The core belief is that the school is not separate from the community it serves, so any person is part of the school regardless of whether they are enrolled.

I love baseball (Go Yankees!), and my favorite day of the Little League Season was always the day we got our uniforms. Our need for identification and social membership, even those who claim to "not join in," always seem to gravitate to like-minded people; thus, their membership is vital. Fred LeBow, credited with starting the Five Boroughs NYC Marathon as President of the NYRRA, once stated, "Never underestimate the power of a free tee-shirt" (Cooper 1992). In the basket, have a shirt for the newest school member and shirts for the parents and guardians. Membership has its privileges, and this is a golden opportunity for the school to "shower" the new parent and child with connection and education.

The process of developing this welcoming basket is multifaceted. Gathering information from community resources (doctors, social service providers, daycare providers, and so on) is also a critical opportunity to develop a robust, proactive, collaborative team to break down and alter preconceived notions of the people and agencies you are involved with. This is not easy; as a result of most of these agencies operating in their separate silos for basically their entire existence, I am including school, turf mentality is alive and well. Engaging in conversation is the easy first step. Still, it must be geared toward structural commitment and driven by a unified philosophy that sound parenting is not separate from sound parenting of a student. Reflection, interviews of parents and students, and constant process re-evaluation and application revision will be the characteristics of a successful program.

The school must immediately assign a counselor to the newborn student's parents to coordinate these efforts. This person is the first key school community member to develop a relationship with the parents. The basket becomes a living resource for the parents and the conduit for two-way education and feedback about the program.

Toddler Orientation

This is where the welcome basket comes alive. Imagine an event where the new parents and their toddlers come into the school and are greeted by people who provided "gifts of knowledge and contacts" to talk through, demonstrate, and provide deeper connectivity to the materials they initially provided. They provide that human touch element to the more profound commitment of caring. Instead of just sitting at tables with various handouts, each group is assigned small groups of parents and toddlers to connect within a rotating schedule sensitive to the parents' and guardians' schedules. Transportation is provided by a community shuttle or some other cooperative arrangement that could include the school transportation system, where permitted. Swag, Stuff We All Get, is plentiful, and Toddler Orientation shirts for toddlers and adults are in the school's colors. Cement the sense of belonging.

As important as it is to have the participants lead the discussions and activities, it is also vital that the school community team ask and listen to see how our parents are doing. The goal is that the parents feel the care and support of the school community so that they are not overwhelmed with the responsibility that we all need them to succeed. Our school community team needs to celebrate their toddlers and their journey. A collaborative needs assessment with the parent, school, and community providers for each Toddler's parent and the school must be created and the domain of the assigned school community/parent team. Think of it as a P.I.E.P. Parent Individual Education Plan. The counselor/mentor will be the P.I.E.P. case manager.

Parent as Primary Teachers Curriculum

Social-emotional, physical, cognitive, psychomotor, and executive functioning skills are the primary needs and skills that all students can benefit from in terms of adjusting to society in general and schooling in particular. We know that all children do not start from the same vantage points and that all children develop not in linear sequence but more akin to an EKG graph. As challenging as it is for teachers to deal with this reality, it is equally so for parents.

Establishing a curriculum for parents to use only makes sense. Instead of relying on some sort of providence to guide parents, based on inventory assessment, available community resources, classroom teachers, and the parents of the students, develop a customizable curriculum that fits your community's unique needs and resources.

The curriculum should be built on specific competencies easily articulated and understood by all the study team players. The needs assessment, the P.I.E.P., and the work with the school counselor-mentor inform the curriculum. It follows then that the parent-issued report card is based on the curriculum. The advantage of the curriculum is that it can become a social contract between families and the school. The guesswork of school readiness is now front and center. Since it is developed in collaboration with the parents, the opportunity to create a co-ownership in the relationship of the student's education is formalized. The social contract reaches beyond the parents and school and includes the community, whose resources and input are vital to success. The curriculum standardizes the needs of the development of the student and gives a clear direction of where the support a family needs to be focused.

Assign a School Counselor/Mentor to Each Parent

Recognizing that each family and child is essential to the school must be represented in a single point of contact. To make the connection between the families and the school the most potent, assign each parent a school counselor/mentor. Whether it is a counselor or mentor, the critical piece is the contact quantity and quality. Quiet classrooms always get my attention; are they quiet because of boredom and complacency, or are they quiet because of engagement and concentration? You only know if you go in there and find out, and that cannot happen to stand on the outside looking in. The same is true for this school counselor/mentor; they must be proactive rather than reactive to keep up with the nature of this approach. Too often, we sit back and become an overwhelmed triage unit rather than investing earlier to offset the more time-consuming and often frustrating reactive responses to student needs. The wellness movement of the last 20-plus years is a prime example of this approach.

The counselor/mentor listens to parents to work with them as they develop and foster a student's needs and help connect and support educational and community service programs for the families. The counselor/mentor plays a key role in the continued evolution of the school community team.

Parent-Issued Report Cards for Their Student

The relationship between the parents is at the heart of affecting the 6 and 18 balance. The core belief is that the parent has the most significant influence as the student's primary teacher and the potential of the most contact time. In respecting this relationship and effectively building upon the team approach with the parent counselor/mentor and the Individual Parent Education Plan (I.P.E.P.), establishing a competency-based progress report card that the parents issue for their children's students can become a powerful tool. This ongoing parent assessment of their student's progress is a powerful way to have direct discussions about their students, needs, growth, and the empowering circumstances for the parent and student. It is also a much more efficient way for the school community to direct assistance and reflect on how their efforts have been influenced. This became the basis of the "Parent School Community Study Team" and the reimagined direction of the New Adult Education Program.

Supporting the Investment

Mentorship and Coaching for Parents

For this section, let us define "mentoring" and "coaching." Mentoring is guiding a parent as their child's primary teacher to interconnect and navigate the parent through their role as the primary teacher based on the mentor's experience and expertise. Coaching is the process of concentrating training and educating on a particular skill or set of skills needed to be an effective educator.

Mentors can be teachers who are also parents, parent volunteers, or school counselors. Particular certifications are optional, but rather a broad set of experiences and a track record of success in guiding students. These mentors are thought partners and confidants committed to bringing out the best in our parent-teachers. Coaches are experts in various skills or skill sets that are wonderful at engaging with one-to-one or small groups. These individuals are incredibly important in creating a "can-do" sense for parent-teachers.

Mentorship is extremely important for parents from the birth of their child up through at least the early grades, and one could argue through 12th grade! Parent-teacher coaching will take on various situations, the re-imagined adult education program, and cooperative professional learning/professional development of classroom and parent-teachers together, students included!

It is interesting to note that in the research from the Wallace Foundation, https://shorturl.at/jkDLY and my work with the NYSED P20 Pilot Program, long-term mentorship and coaching of building and district leaders are cited as necessary in the constant improvement of education leaders. The same is true for parent-teachers.

Re-Imagined Adult Education

Adult education programs need to connect to desired opportunities or identify them as needed if there is any realistic hope for success. Combining adult education with the collaborative needs assessment of the families and the school provides the impetus for feedback and caring that can lead to a robust set of competencies needed for equity success and transforming the 6 and 18 balance continuous growth cycle rather than a chaotic crapshoot.

The programs need to happen at the school; cementing the care relationship is pivotal. Great care for transportation and childcare issues needs to be planned out and provided for; the more hurdles that can be eliminated, the greater the chances for the program's success. The School Community partners: doctors, social service providers, church leaders, and community-based organizations must be not only providers of education but also active supporters. They must commit to the school to this hurdle elimination and actively support and promote adult education.

The school community/parent team leaders need to coordinate the adult education and contact the families. The team must:

- Check-in on how the parent and student are doing and help plan the logistics of the adult education programs.
- Conduct the reflection process and subsequent update of the school's and family's needs assessment.
- Consider what the school community team needs to do to assist the families.
- Consider what educational, social-emotional, and physical?

The school counselor assigned to the parent becomes the focal point of contact between parents and the collaborative school community partners.

Semi-Annual Parent-Teacher PD or PL Fair

The semi-annual parent-teacher PD or PL, professional development or professional learning, fair is an event that pairs parents, students, and the school's teachers in professional training sessions to increase skill sets and approaches for better student education engagement. Bringing together all of the primary players in our education process is essential to the commitment each has to provide for the student. It allows for transparency and recognition of the vital roles each plays in the process and has the opportunity to define those roles and offer real-time assistance. This is the opportunity to speak with one another and listen to challenges to collaborate on what is best for their growing student.

The organization for these "fairs" is best developed along community lines. There are no rules in dividing the fairs by age or grade groups; just work closely with all parties to develop a plan that best suits everyone and remains true to its purpose to strengthen the learning connection beyond the classroom walls. Not all parents will attend, especially if they have multiple work/family commitments. Understanding that not everyone will or can attend, recordings of the events and the opportunity to participate remotely should be aggressively pursued. The essential personal touch central to the effort is follow-up by the counselor/mentor.

Connect with a College/University of the Education Department

Many college and university education preparation programs are always looking for P-12 school partners for placement for their student teachers either in their clinical pre-student teaching phase or final arrangements in the student teaching experience. These preparation programs and student teachers are essential players in this approach, both short and long-term. The experience in working directly with parents and community groups in addition to schools is foundational for connecting the lessons learned in the prep programs and the application in the field. The student teachers and the college/university programs offer an essential element of academic support to the effort. Almost as important, it can put the college/university world in direct contact with families and perhaps future students in a way that is not currently happening on a large scale.

For years, a frequent topic of conversation has been how we can better connect the teacher and administration college/university programs to the P-12 school systems. The stumbling block has usually been how we structurally accomplish the task when the institution has developed that way. This program offers that initial bridge. On the one hand, school districts will need extra help and people to educate their parents. The college/universities have experts and student-teachers in training to offer valuable assistance and gain invaluable experiences. It also serves as a real-time feedback loop to college/university professors regarding the applications and approaches to what they are teaching. This living process can be dynamic and ever-growing in its effectiveness and scope.

What About Foster Care?

Foster care is a vital part of our society today. We need more foster parents to give children an opportunity for support and stability in a world where it is so lacking for them. Foster care is also an arm of the social welfare institution. Regarding the interaction between the administration of its services through the agency and with the school, both groups often need to play in the sandbox better together.

As an administrator, these are the most common problematic interactions I encounter:

- A child is placed in foster care without contact with the school to alert them to the situation.
- The foster parent lives in another school district.
- The child now has to enroll in the new district.
- The social service agency demands that the child be immediately enrolled, not to deny the child's right to a free and public education.
- By law, the school district cannot complete enrollment of a new student without proof of required vaccinations and physicals (depending on the age/grade of the student)— the school district informs the foster parent that the child may not attend until the paperwork is in (in many cases, the child is admitted but a time limit is placed on getting the records to the school district to comply with the law).

The old school district received a request for academic records of a student they needed to be aware was enrolling elsewhere.

The most frustrating part of the all-to-often scenario is that it is unnecessary. Instead of both the agency and school district sitting down and recognizing their legal obligations and, in the spirit of doing what is in the best interest of the student, working out a bureaucratic process that will work for both groups, too often, both sides dig their heels in and simply stick the literal text of the law that was never written or intended to be applied to the foster care situation.

In situations where I have had the most success, my team could sit down with the agency to discuss what was needed. Both sides shared their needs/requirements and the legal pathways they had at their disposal. We would establish a point of contact for the school district and the agency and develop a communication line that worked for both sides. Finally, we would detail the paperwork and timeline both groups could make work and stay in compliance. In cases where this worked and, no, not every time I tried this, did it work, the system flowed, and we could have the least amount of transitional angst as possible for the student and foster parent.

The foster parent is now in the position of the student's primary teacher. The added pressure this can present is that the foster parent often needs more history with the student they are now parenting. Special training and resources must be available to the foster parents before and during their active foster parenting. A separate consideration and set of supportive activities need to be spear-headed by the agency and the school district. It can and should follow the same outline for non-foster parents but recognize the challenges facing foster parenting situations.

Help Create a "Parent-Dream" Researcher

For years, Yale or Harvard University were given credit for conducting a study on the value of writing down specific goals for yourself as a huge advantage for succeeding in meeting those life or career goals. The studies never happened at Yale (1953) or Harvard (1979). However, the persistence of this myth led to a study based on the reported principles of the study to be conducted by the Dominican University. (Retrieved August 6, 2022: https://sidsavara.com/wp-content/uploads/2008/09/researchsummary2.pdf). The premise held that those who wrote down specific goals and reviewed them each day were significantly more likely to achieve those goals than others who did not. It is speculated that there is a subconscious level of commitment when you write down ideas, wishes, and goals but that reviewing those goals, reading, and, in a sense, confronting them guides actions and decisions you make in order to achieve those goals. The more specific or "actionable" you can make those goals, the easier they are to direct your choices.

Aside from the side lesson that you should ALWAYS cross-check what you read on the internet myth of the Yale and Harvard goal-setting studies, the takeaway is still powerful. Students' primary teacher is their parent who, for better or worse, is their tour guide through life as an adult. The student is a captive audience at the experience level of what the parent and school can provide for them in terms of exposure and experiences. As detailed earlier, school, on average, only contributes about 30% of what a student learns, so the burden of exposure and experiences falls on the parent. To see yourself doing something or relating to anything first requires that you are aware, and you cannot be aware if it never existed (in your life) in some way.

Exposure and experiences are the gateway paths for opportunities. With opportunities, the very idea of choices is unlimited. Without support and guidance, the amount of success in expanding opportunities is thwarted. Throughout my education career, many parents supported and encouraged their children to "do their homework." Some even followed that up by screaming at their student and punishing them. While it may have its roots in being well-meaning, this approach often has the opposite effect. Much like the coach who punishes their players by making them run laps for punishment, even though being in good cardiovascular shape is good, the athlete now views running as a punishment. Supporting school work successfully is not to approach it as an act of compliance "you have to do this" but as an overall discovery of who this young person can be and might be; the school work is just exercising tools for success, isolating the tool development to an act(s) of punishment (compliance) and it increases the likelihood of never being used to grow opportunities.

Curiosity, modeling, and encouragement are the mentorship parents can provide to create a powerful launching pad for a student's growth and ability to seek out opportunities. The act of passive and active modeling is powerful. When I coached cross country and track, I noticed that many of my middle-distance runners wore the same brand of running shoes I wore. I then started to see the same phenomena in the more successful programs. Laurie, my wife, and I are voracious readers and writers in my own family. Our daughter, Molly, is pursuing her master's degree in Publishing. We never talked about publishing actively with her as a profession. Still, here she notes: in recent conversations, Molly cites our created environment of family outings to bookstores and excitement of reading and writing as a significant influence. To be actively involved in a student's life is not always easy. A fine line exists between encouraging curiosity and putting pressure to go in particular directions. This is the art of mentorship.

There is no guaranteed prescribed way to be a successful mentor. People, families, circumstances, and particular strengths are all variables that have unique ways to blend, and successful mentoring will need to adjust to all of this all of the time. It is an ever-evolving process. Mentoring and coaching the parent-teachers is vital to keep the pipeline of growing student opportunities alive and well. As much as it is important to support the nitty gritty of academic skill sets and fancy words for homework, it is just and, in many cases, more important to connect to dreams and opportunities. The more a parent can visualize different paths and outcomes for their student, the more ways they will, directly and indirectly, act to keep those dreams alive for their student. That is the key premise when classroom teachers are told to have higher expectations for their students.

Too often, schools spend minimal effort on exposing students to different opportunities (read: career days) to just the students. Therefore, isolating the opportunity experience and not connecting the parents to this information so it can be shared and continued at home to reinforce its value. Schools also concentrate on only what is available locally to ensure representatives show up. What if schools leveraged the internet, such as Zoom, Skype, and Google Meet, integrated the exploration throughout the curriculum, and invited parents to connect into these moments? And what if the schools provided re-imagined adult-student education opportunities to further the engagement and teach how to self-research these pathways? Using digital means to break down physical limitations of exposure to career pathways and opportunities is huge. It also enables parents to connect to these experiences in real-time or delayed recordings that could be viewed on their schedule.

Creating a pipeline of dreams and opportunities is a key experience for parents and their students. Like providing a teacher's curriculum, the dream opportunities help create practical end-game possibilities for the student's educational efforts. After all, this is the premise of focusing on "career and college preparation."

Advertisement, Get the Message Out

I clearly remember in the not-so-distant past that I met resistance from teachers, staff, and parents about giving students email addresses and using Wikipedia. However, encyclopedias were encouraged. Instead, today, almost every district has its web page, Facebook group(s), and text messaging system (usually tied to their "robo-call" system). It may also include its Twitter feed for "live coverage" events. The lesson here is that people love to be connected and want as much communication as possible, and we have a HUGE responsibility to teach digital citizenship.

The majority of core issues all people of all ages have with the current and emerging forms of digital communication is that it is on a four-dimensional platform rather than the three-dimensional face-to-face communication we innately understand. In approximately 1450, Guttenberg invented the printing press, which is largely credited with circulating ideas and amplifying the Renaissance and Enlightenment Periods. This new form of spreading ideas sped up sharing ideas and thoughts. Many more traditional forms of idea-sharing came from the elite classes, church leaders, or political leaders who were questioned and challenged. Those leaders and groups that did not respond to the new realities of communication and idea-sharing were soon vanquished to the sidelines. But, understandably, this evolution took time due to the poor education of most people (most were illiterate) and the cost of the new printed books. As time marched on, the education of the masses improved, and cheaper forms of messaging appeared, namely, the newspaper. It is not surprising that the newspapers were written on the elementary level of reading since elementary schooling was most common, mostly so religious groups could have their congregations read religious texts, and the advent of political cartoons used to advance opinions and deeper interpretation, or is it manipulation of events?

The cycle describes a similar process every time a new communication platform is developed. The speed of the development hinges on the variables of monetizing the platform and its affordability to the masses. The educational impact is in creating more and better researchers of what is out there for consumption. The first and primary education about digital platforms is understanding their interactive nature. Putting something out digitally must be recognized that it does not happen in a closed system. The system is open to give and take comments and challenges with EVERYONE. I often remind educators that their Facebook pages have circulations much larger than the NY Times. Its potential for giving instant feedback can make it an amazing teaching experience.

So, what does all of this information do with advertising our parental-community-education partnership? Everything. First, we must consider and understand the most frequently used platforms of those we intend to reach. Hint: more than using the school website page is needed—most parents view it the same as teacher-written notices sent home. If you are using the school web page, ensure it is the students who are the authors with editing supervision! That way, the parents, grandparents, and anyone else invested in the child will immediately read and share their work. Second, have a broad variety of the platforms you use to reach as many persons as possible. Third, connect all advertisements with the community groups, agencies, and institutions you partner with; think of it as the digital basket you give out to new parents at the start of this partnership relationship. Finally, if there are physical limitations for your parent community accessing digital messaging, fix them, whether it's cost for connections, devices, or understanding how to access. Your voice cannot be heard if they don't connect to it.

Actionable Ideas

Creating a Civic Ecosystem (Poughkeepsie Children's Cabinet-Harvard Ed Redesign Lab)

There are many exciting examples of school districts pulling together parent, community, and school resources to ensure a "cradle-to-career" system of services and support for opportunities and dreams for every one of their students. Poughkeepsie

Children's Cabinet is but one of these inspiring programs that should demand our attention, curiosity, and learning.

The Poughkeepsie program is heavily influenced by its experience as a member of the "By All Means" initiative consortium launched by The Education Redesign Lab (EdRedesign) at the Harvard Graduate School of Education.

Resource Connection: https://edredesign.org/childrens-cabinets (Retrieved December 3, 2022)

Resource Connection: https://www.pkchildrenscabinet.com/ (Retrieved December 3, 2022)

Andragogy-*Tips on Teaching Adult Learners* (From University of San Diego Professional and Continuing Education)

Andragogy is the term used to describe a set of principles, methods, and practices for teaching adult learners. Much of the effort in improving parent engagement is teaching parents and giving them the tools to be their students' primary teachers. Knowing some of the differences between teaching adults rather than students is a good idea.

Children	*Adults*
Rely on others to decide what is important to be learned.	Decide for themselves what is important to be learned.
Accept the information being presented at face value.	Need to validate the information based on their beliefs and experience.
Have little or no experience upon which to draw—are relatively "clean slates."	Have much experience upon which to draw—may have fixed viewpoints.
Expect what they are learning to be useful in their long-term future.	Expect what they are learning to be immediately useful.
Little ability to serve as a knowledgeable resource to teachers or classmates.	Significant ability to serve as a knowledgeable resource to trainers and fellow learners.

Source: The Institute on Aging

Helpful Tips for Working with Parent Mentors

(From Georgia Parent Mentor Partnership—Kim Chester)

INCLUDE parent mentors from the beginning. When parent mentors can work with families early in a student's school years, a true partnership and trust can be developed and maintained. Often, teachers invite a parent mentor to assist in hostile situations or in a student's last year of high school. Parent mentors are most effective when they work to develop strong bonds between family and school from a student's early years.

COMMUNICATE skills that are being taught at school. Parent mentors have opportunities throughout the year to disseminate and reinforce this information to parents in various environments in which the parent and parent mentor interact. In many cases, parent mentors can offer parent training on HOW to incorporate these critical skills in the home and in the community. Many parents do not know how to infuse this information into their daily lives and often need specific training and strategies. In many cases, parents need an opportunity to become aware of these vital strategies.

PARTICIPATE in parent mentor activities. If the parent mentor is offering training or sending information that impacts your students, please take note. This allows the teachers to be informed of parent resources or strategies that may positively impact students. By participating in parent mentor activities, educators communicate their desire to work collaboratively with the families, which often positively impacts the level of trust parents have in the school system.

ENCOURAGE families to include the parent mentor. This tip can go both ways. Often, a parent lacks trust in the school, and parent mentors can work to reestablish trust with the school system. In other situations, parents may not see the need to connect to the parent mentor or may need to understand the purpose of a parent mentor. When trusted educators take the time to explain the purpose and benefits of collaborating with the parent mentor, the team can access more resources and provide a broader base of support for students.

SHARE information with parents. When you receive information and announcements from the parent mentor, please stop and think if that information could be useful to any of your students. If so, please forward the information to the family even if you think the family has received the same information.

By receiving it twice, the parent is more likely to respond or utilize the information.

ACKNOWLEDGE the expertise and experiences of the parent mentor. Parent mentors work to remove barriers to make the team function more effectively. Barriers between home and school occur for many reasons, including a lack of trust due to bad school experiences when the parents were children, not feeling valued as a parent, or feeling all alone and isolated from others. Parent mentors offer a unique connection to parents because they live the life of a parent with special needs. In addition, parent mentors are surrounded by other parents living it as well. This bond between parents is strong and can often move a barrier that seems immovable.

BROADEN your circle of support. Parent mentors work with families daily to find resources for them. This creates a web of crucial supports for our families that are vital to students' success. Parent mentors are often associated with key individuals in family service agencies, mental health clinics, recreational services, independent living supports, transportation resources, etc. In addition, parent mentors are often connected to individuals in the community who might be able to aid in providing internships, employment opportunities, or recreational activities.

Connections-Using Google Classroom

Since its introduction in the fall of 2015, Google Classroom continues to be one of the cheapest, most accessible platforms for parents, teachers, and students to connect directly to the students' classroom environment. Using Google Classroom for guardians' connection, guardians can get weekly or daily emails about their child's progress in the classroom, including grades, missing work, announcements, and connections to as many classes as the student may have that are also using Google Classroom.

Resource Connection-Video: https://www.youtube.com/watch?v=Vl9ofDHkIpE Google Classroom for Guardians—Tutorial (Retrieved December 3, 2022)

Language Learning Apps

(This is not an exhaustive list, NOR is it an endorsement of any kind—if you are interested, I strongly suggest you look to update with the newest applications)

- Duolingo: https://www.duolingo.com/ (Retrieved December 22, 2023)
- Babbel: https://shorturl.at/qszDR (Retrieved December 22, 2023)
- Rosetta Stone: https://www.rosettastone.com/ (Retrieved January 5, 2024)
- Lingodeer: https://www.lingodeer.com/ (Retrieved January 5, 2024)
- Memrise: https://www.memrise.com/en-us/ (Retrieved January 8, 2024)
- Busuu: https://www.busuu.com/ (Retrieved January 8, 2024)
- Hello talk: https://www.hellotalk.com (Retrieved January 9, 2024)
- Tandem: https://www.tandem.net (Retrieved January 10, 2024)
- Beelinguapp: https://beelinguapp.com (Retrieved January 10, 2024)
- Speechling: https://speechling.com (Retrieved January 13, 2024)

Rules for Educating Parents
PARENT PARTNERSHIP IS THE PATH TO EQUITY OF DREAMS

By definition, a partnership is a form of business where two or more people share ownership and the responsibility for managing the company and the income or losses the business generates.

Despite the misguided and dangerous prognostications of politicians and education leaders who should know better, our education system is built upon providing opportunities, not guaranteeing outcomes. The greatest tool you have as an administrator is your ability to educate. By taking on the leadership role of a school district, it is your professional obligation to create, promote, and help provide opportunities for your students. That means upgrading facilities, reviewing and revising curriculum to higher and better standards, figuring out ways to connect and engage more students, teaching and leading accountability, and finally, it means, for many students, changing the 18:6 ratio.

The 18:6 ratio is the quiet but substantial reason why education alone only marginally assists students in having better opportunities than their parents. Students are in our care at school for an average of six hours a day; the other 18 hours a day are spent elsewhere, ideally under the supervision of an adult or parent. If the parents are motivated, have means, and have had positive experiences with education. There is a high degree of likelihood that the lessons taught at school academically and socially are being reinforced, and the students' opportunities are at the forefront of interest from the adults; the students feel the importance. Suppose the student is in a home where the parents struggle to make ends meet or have not had a positive experience at school or since their schooling years. In that case, the likelihood that the academic and social lessons from a school are being reinforced and the students' opportunities are at the forefront of interest from the adults is not likely. The student is living in two separate worlds that do not connect. The parents do not understand any positive feelings by the student, nor often notice. Frustration sets in by both the student and parents, and it becomes easier, in a sense, for the student to have negative feelings about school and its opportunities because those whom the child is with 18 hours a day feel the same way. It is the passive expectation that is being reinforced.

In many cases, the only way to break down this cycle is to get the student more involved with the school beyond the regular school day. After-school activities, clubs, sports, and extra educational opportunities provide the vehicle to extend those six average hours and start to tip the balance of time spent in positive academic and social opportunities.

PARENTS NEED TO BE INFORMED, AND IT MUST BE EVERYONE'S RESPONSIBILITY

Knowing and understanding the community is the compass leaders need to connect.

Strange things happen in schools when it comes to parent communication. Many educators often feel they are damned if they do and damned if they don't. If they do inform a parent(s) of their child's progress, complaints about not seeing their child in a positive light are messages I hear. They will hear about the lack of communication if they fail to inform parents. How to decide is easy; which of the following headlines can you live with: (1) "The school is overwhelming me with information"; and (2) "The school never tells me anything about how my child is doing and when they do it's always too late to do anything and it's negative"?

It is not hard to understand; a child psychologically represents their best effort in life to a parent. It is also true that, unlike our faculty and staff, our children mostly only have one shot at each grade, so every year, every day, is their most important at that time.

In education, we are a primary social service industry. Therefore, our customer service skills are essential in determining our success. Our customers are not the parents but the students; this is our focus. Many parents and others will argue the implications of this point; however, this is the heart of the connection of our soft skills and eliminating barriers to engagement. Parents and guardians need multiple modalities to get and collaborate information with our administration, faculty, and staff. Many need to be versed in the digital world, and some in our rural areas do not even have the opportunity to be connected. Know your audience. If you still have to rely on pre-digital methods, be creative and create opportunities for information to flow both ways.

Often, when leaders talk about two-way communication in education, it falls on the shoulders of the school community members. I do not believe this is right. We need to demand and give our parents and guardians permission to interact all the time, not just send reports home and only receive information when the parent has a question or problem. It places the school in the impossible position of proving a negative; that is not productive.

Administrators lead and provide professional development to our faculty and staff; the same care must happen to our parents and guardians. If we commit to the idea that the best situation for a student is when the school's and the home's efforts are in line and equally in support in the form of a societal compact, then we must make sure our communication structure matches our aim. Aside from providing primary professional development for parents (think the open house, adult education, and library classes), we must also ask parents what they need. This resolve must come from all levels of our school community, from the classroom, cafeteria, music, art, athletics, and central office.

CONNECTIONS ARE IMPORTANT OPPORTUNITIES

I have always connected to history; it is why I majored in it at college and went on to teach history in the classroom for 18 years before I moved into administration. For me, history is our community's genetics and creates the frames of reference for how schools operate. Honoring and understanding your school's history is half of the equation; understanding how it is alive in the fabric of what you see and experience today is your advanced degree. To do this, you need to become part historian and part sleuth (I would write Columbo, but I fear many would not get the TV character reference).

Understanding the historical fiber of the district is to understand the context of the current state of affairs. This knowledge provides the tools you need to seek out the knowledge or experience that will move the district forward more efficiently. Recognizing the areas of either knowledge or expertise you need is the soft skill that leadership demands. Connecting and maintaining those relationships often translate to more opportunities and growth for you, your team, and your students.

Many leaders forget why they took the time to learn the history (read: Context) of the current state of affairs. The administrator must use that piece of the puzzle to bring the opportunities in a manner that it is your team's idea, not yours. The engagement and ownership from the start must be your team's and students'. No exceptions. Opportunities are ideas waiting for a productive outcome. Seek out the connections, build with those committed to the current state, and foster their ownership of the newer directions; the opportunities will abound.

> **Reflection**
>
> 1 Describe which community programs that exist where you live that you believe should be a part of a school community partnership.
> 2 From your experience, which competencies would you include on a parent-issued report card on their student? Age 2–3; 4–5; 6–7

Additional Resources

DeWitt, P. M. (2018). *Coach it further: Using the art of coaching to improve school leadership.* Corwin Press.

https://shorturl.at/jkDLY (Retrieved December 3, 2023).

https://sidsavara.com/wp-content/uploads/2008/09/research summary2.pdf (Retrieved August 6, 2022).

https://youtu.be/Vl9ofDHkIpE (Retrieved December 3, 2022).

References

Berliner, D. C., & Glass, G. V. (Eds.). (2014). *50 myths and lies that threaten America's public schools: The real crisis in education.* New York, Teachers College Press.

Cooper, P. L. (1992). The "Visible Hand" on the footrace: Fred Lebow and the marketing of the Marathon. *Journal of Sport History, 19*(3), 244–256.

5

Creating Opportunities

The Traditional View

Teachers and administrators often discuss that many children are better served by staying with us in school than returning home right after the traditional school day ends. A good friend and administrator, David Anderson, once said we are only "a meal and bed away from being an orphanage." We then darkly conclude that it might not be the worst outcome. Please allow me to be clear; I am NOT advocating that we should become such a facility. Still, perhaps in extreme situations, putting some safeguards in place could be a respite alternative for those families (Monday-Friday) in dire circumstances. I do think that would be worth some consideration.

To extend the traditional six-hour day, many schools simply extended the hours of their day; others tack on clubs, activities, and sports programming. This is done to attract students to positive activities and keep their interest. The result is often an eclectic array of offerings and opportunities that represent the volunteers and traditional offerings with only indirect or no connections to a unified program or community, parent wishes, thoughts, or ideas. Although the best intentions are present, their effectiveness is stunted due to the design.

Extracurricular

Extracurricular: ex·tra·cur·ric·u·la/ˌekstrəkəˈrikyələr Adjective: (of activity at a school or college) pursued in addition to the ordinary course of study.

In its original form, the term extracurricular was to provide practical and vocational opportunities to students who needed to be more practical during the ordinary course of study during the school day. The idea was to create opportunities to take the knowledge they were (hopefully) amassing in the classroom and have a practical platform to pursue further and develop it. Progressive educators during the late 20th and early 20th centuries saw this as the natural extension of preparing the incubation of the next society. Powerful ideas assumed that everyone in society saw opportunities in similar ways. There was no connection or consideration of what parents and the community thought of what the next or growing society should be; this was the domain of the schooling community. Think of it as the trickle-down theory of education. The more education you can deliver, even though you know those on the top of the food chain will have the best advantage. Still, because of the sheer volume, the result will be greater for everyone, though not equally, and with no discernible effect on leveling the playing field. The problem is that while all benefit from a net increase on a gross scale, it still structurally promulgates the stratified opportunities and position in that society. The idea of a fluid class structure or meritocracy has institutional barriers; some are intended, while others result from de facto circumstances.

The ultimate guide of any undertaking is purpose. Education is no different in that regard. Even if something has a stated purpose, some will buy into it. "Hey teach, why do we have to do this? Because the state says you will be tested on it so we have to do it." That is not the most compelling argument. We take the heart out of motivation when we do things simply for compliance's sake (Pink, 2011). I suggest Daniel Pink's work, *Drive: The Surprising Truth About What Motivates Us*. When parents and students can understand and feel the connection to what schools are doing both during the day and before or after school extracurriculars, what was once just six-hour support grows.

Connect After-School Work to School Day Work
The progressive education movement of the late 19th and early 20th century had this principle at the forefront of their belief that through education as the incubation processor, we constantly can develop a process of an ever more evolved and better society. The mechanism of the process may be valid, but without the partners (parents, students, teachers, community), shared belief, commitment, and vision of undertaking its success are limited.

How to Grow Those Traditional Programs
Many of the traditional programs that schools already offer are a great starting point. It comes down to the programs' connection with the families and seeing how it fits their needs as the teacher-parent. Adjusting programming offerings and leveraging community and parent resources to fit the needs of the families directly are critical for the support and growth of the students. To have the parents as active participants adds to the program's shared ownership.

Keeping the dream of what parents want for their children alive is a crucial internal motivation. The only way to do this is to cement relationships, listen, and assist with removing possible barriers. This is where the connection and team approach of the larger community that serves the people of the school community comes into focus. Balancing the family's needs logistically and structurally at home to support the student child and parents, who have only one place to have a relationship with and connect to these resources, is pivotal in measuring effectiveness and coordinating efforts. For too long in our current model, non-education entities have attempted to coordinate assistance without the main focus being supporting the student child and the one pathway that can change the next generation. The Parent, Guardian School Community Study Team is key to coordinating efforts.

Focus on Questioning Skills
The idea of affecting the 6 and 18 balance is to educate people about possibilities and opportunities coupled with their engagement and ownership of the responsibility. If we want to educate

more effectively and live up to one of the most overused school mission statements of all time, "...*to develop lifelong learners*..." we ought to understand how that happens and what skills to develop, whether we are talking about students or their parents. To own one's education, the student or parent must become the researcher. Individuals with a robust skill set as researchers develop curiosity and internal motivation for growth. We must develop better questioning skills for our students and parents and facilitate their skills in source acquisition. Asking better and more profound questions ultimately results in more satisfying answers.

Instead of delivering answers to questions and evaluating growth based on the regurgitation of the answers, focus on investigating solutions. That all starts with questioning skills.

Ideas Need the Connection-Resources

The extracurricular offerings must be mapped out with the same care of construction our curriculums aspired to be. The process is straightforward: follow the data, assess the needs and trends, and strategize how best to support. The structure is the key to staying within the system and developing the offerings. To have the P.I.E.P., parent-issued child report card, and the Parent, School Community Study Team, a school community team has all the data points to establish a strong foundation of the needs assessment to direct extracurricular offerings. Categorizing the needs as Wellness: food, clothing, shelter, active playtime; Academic: study skills, quiet setting/space, interest expansion/expression; and Community Connections: local experiences, regional experiences, global experiences, and any others that the trends dictate will significantly facilitate the process.

Once the needs are categorized (reminder: the process needs to be inclusive with all partners, especially parents), the work of organization and connection to what is happening in the classroom curriculums is the next step; the Progressive Reformers were on to something; they just missed the powerful opportunity of including the primary teacher parents.

Ideas for Programming

Summer Enrichment/Teach Using Community Resources

As superintendent, I visited our elementary and middle school summer school sessions on my first day. At dismissal, I found myself with a group of teachers lamenting the challenges of getting these students to pass (the requirement to be in summer school then was that you failed during the school year) despite this "extra opportunity" afforded by having summer school. I asked the gathering if they used the same teaching methods during the regular school year. They looked at me as if I had lost my mind. I suggested that if they stepped back and saw that using the same approach but expecting different outcomes was kind of crazy, maybe they could be open to figuring out what the student's disconnection was. This conversation is the wrong approach on your first day on the job as their leader. I did not recognize that they were not there to hurt or further kill off a student's drive for success; quite the opposite. They were there because they were committed to the students and wanted to see them succeed.

Based on this inauspicious first encounter and a series of lengthy conversations with my Elementary Principal, Melinda McCool, we decided to change summer school and what it meant. We both agreed that the current "traditional" model did not effectively work. It was viewed as punishment and public embarrassment to "extra" school. We changed our administration of the program and approach. Our summer school became our summer enrichment program, emphasizing community connections and engagement. Our classes would design a theme for the summer. The students would collaboratively work on a final project that could take any form imaginable, from a digital presentation, video, or theatrical performance, to name a few. We still targeted and strongly encouraged parents of students who were academically struggling to attend but ensured the opportunity was open to everyone. We also included bus transportation to the three major day camps in our served towns once our school let out at 11:30. The result was a tremendous uptick of all students enrolling and taking advantage of the program. When a grant was available for our CROP, Creating Rural Opportunity Program, our transition to its summer program was seamless since we had already laid the groundwork.

In retrospect, if we had enveloped the program with an integrated parent approach, it would have only amplified the successes we had enjoyed. The lesson from our experience was clear: the more we connected with the community, the more involved our growing village became. The next logical step is to integrate these opportunities.

 **Actionable Ideas**

Extended Day
CROP The Creating Rural Opportunities Partnership (CROP) After School and Summer Program is a consortium funded by two successful grant applications for the federally funded 21st Century Community Learning Centers program. The grant awards run for five years. Continued funding is contingent on federal budget approval. This federally funded program has four primary goals: to grow citizens who contribute positively to their communities. The pillars of this goal focus on Academic Support, Youth Development (to help students grow into positive citizens through enrichment such as community-based service learning, arts, clubs, technology, nutrition classes, field trips, recreation and games, and visits from community organizations; and Family Engagement (Connecting families to their child's education through family nights and workshops and providing links to other helpful community supports).

The powerful aspect of this program is how it goes beyond the traditional school year to include the summer. Its intentions and efforts are dead on what we have been discussing; however, it is often left to be a stand-alone program despite its grand vision. The compelling aspect of these opportunities is listening to its ardent supporters who express anecdotal evidence of its positive impact on students. Full disclosure: In the school district where I was a superintendent, we have this program, and its popularity among parents and teachers was, at times, overwhelming.

Despite these positive vibes, the other side of the program was the tremendous work that the coordinator and facilitators had to put into the program to ensure success and its continuing march to achieving its goals. Many of those involved get burned out and realize the incredible amount of time and effort is only possible if you teach all day and do this right after the traditional school day. My point is that if a school district has the structure around this program and this program is a tool for the goals it has rather than proffered as the "solution," its effect can become amplified. Much of the coordination of its efforts can spread out to the process and parent counselor, The Parent, Guardian School Community Study Team, and the redesigned Adult Education Program.

This kind of program and the parent structure should be available wherever needed; it is needed everywhere, whether rural, suburban, or urban. Equity challenges are abundant wherever you find socio-economic challenges, minorities, and families with language challenges. These challenges are amplified if the family is black or brown and has English-speaking challenges. Coordination, structure, and a comprehensive curriculum remain the linchpin to success.

The Capstone Project Program-Identify Local/Community Problems

One of the core pieces of ownership is the ability to identify an issue and positively affect a change. The dynamic of 6 and 18 is understanding and validating the primary teacher role of parents, growing the relationship, and supporting the parents, students, teachers, and the community's dreams for the next generation. Integration of these ideas and efforts comes from a common sense and commitment to address our community collaboratively and affect change.

Becoming a better listener and researcher develops a more robust approach to identifying challenges and becoming involved with their solution(s). This approach should be the mainstay of our entire education system for students and their parents. Self-advocacy becomes more than just "give me something" and more of "give me the pathway to address this issue and the resources to make it better."

What this can look like in a school program is limitless. Imagine it as part of a graduation requirement, an alternative or in addition to "community service" requirements, or perhaps, to comply with the CDOS, career development, and occupational Studies, requirements that many states now demand of its students either as an alternative or outright condition of graduation.

Community Internship
Several ways can replicate a community internship program to further interest and meet the needs of students and the larger communities they ultimately affect. The district I led offers one such program in conjunction with Wise Services. From their website (https://www.wiseservices.org/wise-program/), the description states:

> A WISE program enables high school seniors of all ability levels to design an individualized, passion-driven project. Projects can include, but are not limited to, internships, independent research, self-improvement, community service, or cultural, artistic, and performance-based activities. The topics students can explore in school-based, experiential learning programs are limitless.

The primary goal is to give the student a powerful pathway to use their academic skills to research and formulate an internship cooperatively designed with the student and person-in-field mentor who agrees to work with the student in their exploration. Along with the internship, review research, journaling of the experience, an ultimate capstone project and public presentation of the experience. Our district made an in-house curricular choice for high school seniors to substitute part of their 12th-grade English and Social Studies class by taking this program.

While I support the WISE Services Program and have firsthand experienced its power for students, any school can run a very similar program given the support and structure needed to coordinate and recruit needed "in-the-field" mentors. The program's power lies in the student's ownership of the experience and the commitment between the student and the community field mentor. Developing a competency-based program for the internship experience facilitates the backward planning of the academic components and research expectations and the concrete structure of the program to meet the individual's schedule.

Pre-Pre K

Many school districts in the Northeast corridor of the United States are experiencing declining populations and enrollment. This increases the per-student costs of education. The situation presents a challenge for the community's financial resources. It is a challenge for schools to provide the education we depend upon for our long-term growth as a society (however you define that ideal). During the general growth period of the post-WWII era, known as the "baby boomer" generation, many schools expanded their capacities to meet the growing population's needs. Today, we are faced with maintaining the aging buildings and or considering shuttering the facilities that once served our youth. This is not an easy task. While some in the community understand the realities of a shrinking population and the rising costs of hanging on to those buildings, others are too emotionally attached. When communities consider merging schools and districts, the meetings can be more charged than Wrestlemania events. In school administration, we call this the "killing of the mascot," though even thinking of changing a mascot's name or image can bring similar emotions! The result is that school districts work through alternatives short of the "m" merging word and sell communities on ideas of shuttering buildings as needed. Another path is the redesigning of the existing buildings beyond their traditional services.

A concept that I find interesting is the repurposing of classroom space to help meet one of the most common needs of many communities—affordable daycare. Dr. Lester Young, the current chancellor of the New York State Board of Regents, recently at a meeting commented on how we do not concentrate our efforts at equity in educating our youth early enough—citing that research establishes the window of learning of children before the age of four is so essential. Yet, schools are not a player in this period.

Many schools have the extra classroom space to open up a Pre-PreK program in either cooperation with existing vendors in the community or with local family service agencies. School buildings already meet all the building codes for such facilities and offer the additional benefits of digital connection, cleaning services, and cafeterias. It also allows bringing into focus all of the early intervention strategies we discussed earlier, not to mention the possibility of a robust and coordinated curriculum and community efforts.

College and Career Experience—No, NOT Another Fair!

One of the biggest oversights in our PK-12 schools is sheltering or addressing with our students and their families the outcomes of their education when they are 11th-grade students. It seems as though we (collective "we") operate on the premise that if we start challenging or exploring with children the path they should follow before 11th grade, we will somehow "limit" their opportunities. We have greatly diminished their opportunities by not addressing them before 11th grade. The exception to this process is with our special education students. They, by law, must have a continuing developing plan for the after-graduation period in their life from the time they are 15 years old, called the Secondary Transition Plan. We need to develop transition plans for all of our students, and the process must start at the start of schooling, not the middle or tail end. Leveraging natural curiosity, exposure, and the ability to dig deeper into opportunities and visualize paths to pursue cannot be done in the 18 months we now effectively use with our students when they turn 16 years old.

I envision integrating our curriculum with career exposure and experience with ALL grades. Include parents and community members as participants and co-explorers, whether we do it remotely or simply student-produced videos of the experience. We know from our life that occupations, careers, and professions are not separate from the associated lifestyles of those who pursue these opportunities; rather than shield our students and, by extension, their parents from these opportunities, we need to demonstrate in a real-world way the connection of the work we do in the classroom with the work in the post-school world.

College visitations and on-campus experiences have been ongoing in various capacities for a long time. They can prove hugely important for many students but are even more critical for the parents. Parents who do not benefit from the first-hand experience of going to college and, more importantly, understand the confounding experience of the process are less likely to assist and lead their children. And, no, I am not advocating that every child must go to college. However, every child is entitled to make an informed decision as to whether or not going to college is a proper fit for their chosen path. We further know that if parents are not able, by their experiences or knowledge, to guide, lead, and support their child, de facto, whether or not to go to college is not an option. That is simply not fair.

I explained earlier in the book that despite my parents' lack of direct experience with college, they saw it as a requirement for their children to have that pathway. It still did not make it easier for them and me to understand the process. For full disclosure, my sisters and I, attended a private college prep curriculum high school that supported my parents' aspirations. Still, having this structure in place, I vividly recall my parents' fears in understanding a foreign process to them and myself as a student. There were many arguments about what must be done, when, and even how to choose a college. I was getting the student side of information from well-meaning guidance counselors. My parents were piecing together snippets of conversations with friends and relatives who were well-meaning but had different filters and experiences directing their pontifications and advice. In conclusion, even the best-structured schools for this path can come up short when parents are not aggressive and, over the k-12 time, are educated on the process and its possibilities.

Imagine a process integrated from the early grades onward to what college and career prep programs can offer along with the career-connected curriculum. In a small, bite-sized but consistent manner so that, in the end, an informed decision that respects their dreams and desires is not hindered by the "inside" knowledge usually reserved for those of more privileged circumstances.

Teacher Pipeline

Enrollment in New York's teacher education programs has declined by roughly 50 percent since 2009. At the same time, the state Teacher Retirement System projects that one-third of the state's teachers could retire in the next five years. SUNY projects that New York will need 180,000 teachers in the next decade. There also is a pressing need to diversify the teaching workforce. While 43 percent of students statewide are Hispanic/Latinx or African-American, just 16 percent of the teachers are.
(https://www.nysut.org/news/2020/december/media-release-student-teachers)

The concerns continue when we look at the current enrollment figures for teacher preparation programs 2015–2016 = 41,883: White = 54%, Latin/Hispanic = 14%, African-American = 10%, Latin/Hispanic & African-American = 24% (Source: Title II Higher Education Act). To further exacerbate the situation, in New York State, as in many other states, a person must first be a qualified and practicing teacher to qualify to be a building or district-level administrator. Thus, for many of our students, few, if any, persons are their teachers or administrators who look like them, can easily relate to their experiences, and feel comfortable interacting and depending on them for guidance, learning, advice, and general relationship-building.

I am continually impressed by the pragmatic and progressive approaches athletic coaches have taken throughout the 20th Century to promote and recruit more successfully than the traditional academicians. The latter often deride sports as something of a lesser pursuit and in direct opposition to the "purity" of academia. When I was coaching XC and track and later when my daughter was recruited, I experienced firsthand how the recruitment process plays out. Coaches know the type of student-athlete they want; they look for those types of students and then contact them and, during the process, eliminate as many hurdles as possible to secure the commitment to attend their institution. We need the same active commitment from College/University Teacher Prep Programs. Professors in these programs must accept responsibility for their preparation program, the institution they serve, and their ethical commitment to the profession. I know those are strong charges, but let us face it. Now, the time is to stop lamenting the situation and learn from our athletic departments about their commitment to building and maintaining the competitive programs we desperately need.

PK-12 schools should be partners in this process. When I was in High School (and no, we did not write on clay tablets, but we did have real slate chalkboards!), there was an active Future Teachers of America Club. Sadly, these clubs do not exist any longer; however, the descendant of FTA does, Educators Rising. The Urban League could also be a powerful partner in explicitly reaching out to and supporting students (future education leaders) of color. Consider combining the opportunities that Educator Rising and the Urban League offer. Add active recruitment by teachers and the college teacher prep programs. Bring students into teacher professional development sessions as participants alongside our current teachers. The need is to develop partnership programs with college/university teacher prep programs. Offer college in HS classes for college credit and guarantee admission to teacher prep program if the student performs well in courses taught in high school. And actively seek out grants and financial aid for these opportunities. Never waste the opportunity a crisis presents!

Extended Education
- Vot-Tec teacher pipeline training—taking people already in the field and creating a program that leverages transition teacher certification routes
- Connection with Labor Union Temples pre-apprentice and apprentice programs
- Career Center Program

Digital Minions
Remember the old "AV Squad?" It is time to return to the updated version. The old AV squads ran the 16mm projectors and film strip projectors for teachers, classes, and assemblies. (Check out the glossary for definitions of those terms!). We believe that active

engagement in education is key to learning. Having students as partners with teachers in the structure of the classrooms and delivery of the lesson only makes sense. This was brought home when my daughter started her Fall 2020 semester. The college recruited undergraduates to be "multi-modality assistants" (I prefer my "Digital Minions" title). This was a direct response to the situation many schools found themselves in. Some students chose to be in in-person classes, while some of the classes were remote at the same time. The student workers assisted professors in coordinating their cameras (Zoom, Google Meet, FaceTime, etc.) and online platforms. This arrangement provides real-time feedback between the students and teachers on what works, what could be done better, and how to be directly involved in the process. I think this can quickly happen and should happen on the PK-12 level.

More Ideas

- Flexible Learning Spaces: make the resources of the school open for both students and parents after school
- Host workshops or events that involve parents in the child's education
- Offer adult education classes for both parents alone and parent-child classes after school
- Health and Wellness Programs with community partners for parents and students
- Coding classes or robotics clubs to extend STEAM programming
- Community Service and Volunteer Opportunities—further Community Partnerships
- Collaborate with local businesses for hands-on learning experiences
- Language and Cultural Programs: Offer language immersion programs or cultural exchange activities. Provide opportunities for students to explore and appreciate different cultures
- Provide Grants to encourage flexible club programming.

Rules for Creating Opportunities
If It Isn't Broke, Why Not Break It
A few years ago, I was sitting with my elementary principal, Melinda McCool, and she remarked that one of the puzzling things she frequently dealt with was giving "permission" to the faculty and staff to make changes. At this time, we were challenging our faculty, staff, and students to integrate technology to enhance all levels of engagement for students, parents, and our support staff. We adopted the unofficial credo, "If it isn't broke, why not break it." At faculty meetings and professional development, we highlighted our pioneers and set them up to be our go-to individuals to share their experiences and made it a group share.

One of my first significant reflections on teaching (it also goes for administration!) was my observation that during the first three to five years of a teacher's, or administrator's, career, they will do their best and most awful teaching and leading. The reason is simple: there are no past experiences to get in the way of guiding their imagination and enthusiasm. Once experience and creativity are forced to be more efficient; the risk-taking and uninhibited expressions become muted. The result is actions that have far more to do with getting through and complying rather than exploring.

A whole industry has quietly developed to offset this reality. Goal-setting reflective exercises are all tools to keep innovation and improvement momentum. These tools are useful but lack the challenge and newness of the uninhibited new person. Therefore, organizations (schools) need to create a climate that pursues internal stability while at the same time cherishing the new-person view of possibility. The leader has to model the "why not break it" mentality and be willing to do it themselves with their BOEs.

Think Tomorrow and Work on It Now
The duality of thinking tomorrow and working on it today is a cellular part of excellent educators. It is the genesis of backward planning. Tying this visionary approach to facilities and

grounds and the education mission necessitates a 360-degree view of regulations, operations, human resources, and timing and a rudimentary knowledge of engineering and architecture. It is no wonder your relationship with facilities and grounds will be close. Otherwise, you risk constantly trying to play catch up and, in the process, burning out many human and financial resources that the district needs help with recovering. Planning, reviewing, updating, and assigning tasks must become a regular part of your leadership team. These simple actions will go a long way to ensuring a smooth and cohesive physical structure.

Pride is the ultimate expression of necessary arrogance. To be successful at anything, the school district must have this feeling of confidence that their school stands for excellence. Attention to detail in its appearance and function is the lag indicator of its success.

The facilities determine what its human resources can leverage to move thoughts, ideas, and actions forward. Care of the physical plant frees up economic and labor resources (it is far more efficient to maintain a facility than constantly repairing one), so other investments are possible.

A well-designed school can offer many choices for students that enhance its educational and extracurricular programs and keep its people safe. Matching form and function should always be at the forefront of the leadership team's planning and maintenance discussions. If you build it, they will use it.

It's about Serving Students Now

It is important to keep our school connected to its past, especially its successes and what makes it unique. However, only some of what has happened previously falls into that category, thus making it our task to discern which categories apply. In the words of Alan November, "we need to be in the learning business and get out of the school business." We exist to guide and develop learning experiences for our students. Everything else is either complementary or non-essential. Too often, we are held back by what we have done in the past for no practical reason other than that we are comfortable with it.

Our students today and their needs must be our focus. We are in a service industry, and our customer service is to the students and their learning needs. Our facilities and grounds are the physical structures that we have to create learning environments that are dynamic and equipped appropriately to carry out the mission. Students need to be a part of this process; their interaction and voices are data that you need to make thoughtful decisions.

Logistics and Structure, the Twin Pillars of Sanity

Sanity is underappreciated by many in the education community. One look at the number of laws and regulations we must comply with for our education charge will make many just shake their heads. I have an unsupported inclination that this might be the origin of those developing our unique language of acronyms in education. All jokes aside, the manager's skill set of handling and understanding logistics and how to implement structures to facilitate them is the key to keeping your sanity, especially in training BOE members.

As hard as it may be to imagine, many BOE members have lives outside of school; some even have other jobs! Setting up a structure that supports and lends strength to the how, what, and when of information, events, invitations, and official business is key to keeping your mind open.

For example, do you have structure and strategies for the following?

1. Death of an important person in the community, parent, staff/faculty member;
2. Remembrance for a past employee or BOE member;
3. Getting daily news flashes out about ANYTHING;
4. Practices to allow (or not allow) board members to enter the school;
5. Disseminating news;
6. Expectations of how the members are to react to news requests for interviews or answering questions;
7. Liaisons to various groups (SPTO, Booster Club, and so on);

8   Protocols of social media expectations;
9   In-service state education updates and professional development.

The list is far from complete, but it aims to push you along the path of your professional field of vision. A plan with no planning is not a plan at all. It is important to get help.

Use your formal and informal associations to get into conversations about the seen and unforeseen, especially when you are a new superintendent. You can't anticipate all situations; however, many of the same situations raise their heads from time to time everywhere. Learning is messy, but you can still clean up before you are a mess! The informal and formal connections you create are your greatest resource. Sanity is important.

If It Works, What Is Your Plan to Improve On It?

Nothing in schools can remain stagnant. Buildings and grounds require maintenance year-round. Summer break is more for your building than anything else; it is the only downtime that the plant has to recover and repair.

Working cooperatively with whoever is in charge of facilities and grounds management is essential. A coordinated plan that considers planned and unplanned maintenance and repairs is a primary component of your strategic planning. There should be a plan to improve efficiency and updates. Require your facilities and grounds person or people to research and recommend these undertakings regularly and give them permission and encouragement. Making budget choices is difficult, but the mantra "pay now, or pay more later" does apply. Obviously, during tight fiscal times, it will not always be the easiest or most practical item to invest in, but the more you can do, the better off your district will be later on.

The one word that drives everything in education is the purpose. For facilities and grounds, this means functionality and durability. Connecting the functionality and durability to the goals and mission of the school district is primary to the plan for learning. Again, it becomes a matter of balancing priorities and investment resources. Unfortunately, many states mandate municipalities, such as schools, operate on the premise of the lowest bid. Projects over a threshold amount of money must be sent out for bid, and the person or company that formally offers to complete the task, according to the specifications, at the lowest rate must be accepted unless a reason for disqualification exists. Though not always the case, more often than not, you get what you pay for. Therefore, in assembling the specifications, it becomes critical to consider the budget and every detail that goes into the project to ensure a level and standard of quality.

> **Reflection**
>
> 1. Other than school sports teams, what after-school programs do you know of that have been successful? Why have they been successful? How did students who were part of the program gain more than those who had not? How do you measure the success of the students?
> 2. Design the before or after-school program you would like to see; explain the elements you envision vital to the program's success.

Additional Resources

Emery, M. E. (1990). *The partnerships project: Linking educational opportunity and community development to revitalize rural communities into global villages*. Final Report.

Pink, D. H. (2011). Drive: The surprising truth about what motivates us. Penguin: New York.

References

https://www.nysed.gov/curriculum-instruction/cdos-pathway-regents-or-local-diploma (Retrieved December 4, 2023).

https://www.wiseservices.org/wise-program/ (Retrieved December 4, 2023).

https://www.nysut.org/news/2020/december/media-release-student-teachers (Retrieved December 4, 2023).

6

Teacher-Administrator-School Community Leadership

Accepting the Need: Defining the Equity Issue for Everyone

Accepting the ramifications of the 6 and 18 balance and its role in the inequity of our education system takes work. In a real sense, it is the death of our education reality. Many of us have grown up with the myth that having an opportunity to show up and perform was enough because it was no longer "separate but equal" and that the playing field, if not perfect, was far more equal than it was in the past; this is untrue. While the trappings appear somewhat similar, the abilities to access the resources and develop along a seamless childhood to adolescent growth are rife with detours, dead ends, and hurdles. There is no getting around the mystery of the situation. Education equity is really about community equity. At the core is a lack of wealth and resources when you add in the extra layers of racism, both intentional and by design, and the de facto result of a structure made to fit a middle and upper-class system. The system has its guiding structural principles of belief that are not universal or even aware that it exists. The result is what we have: an incredible opportunity whose doors are closed to our people who need them the most.

Accepting this reality is about recognizing the stages of grief we inevitably have to experience to start rebuilding our schools to support equity and move the 6 and 18 balance in a way that can work together and not in isolation from each other. The stages are familiar:

DENIAL: We do not have an equity education problem; they must apply themselves.
ANGER: Our school is not perpetuating inequity.
BARGAINING: If the state gave us more money, we could do something about it.
DEPRESSION: It is hopeless; without money, or even if we had it, how can we fix everything?
ACCEPTANCE: We believe our children to be our legacy of a better tomorrow; we have to do what we can to help parents connect with our opportunities and educate them about their role as much as we educate the children.

The Acceptance phase is critical to allow our school leaders and administrators to build a vision to action that accepts the key to turning the 6 and 18 balance into a force of equity and opportunity in educating the parents about their primary roles. Only when we accept this reality and have parents understand their pivotal roles can their decisions about their student child's futures be fully respected and supported.

A Thoughtful Balance between Information/Advocacy/Guiding/Opportunities

Case Study

Pat's mother sits at the table with Pat across from Principal Higgins. The principal led the discussion over Pat's latest discipline event and concluded that Pat needs more services and will receive a three-day out-of-school suspension with three hours of tutoring per day. Pat's mother scoffs at the pronouncement and states, "you are just giving Pat three days off, that won't fix anything." The principal, who has been in education a long time, responds:

> The effect of the out of school suspension is on you and what you choose to do, say, and react with your child. This time away from school is a chance for both of you to work together to straighten out the behaviors and reconnect to what is important. Meanwhile, our teacher needs to reset the rest of the classroom to ensure that the interruption does not have any lasting impact on everyone else's right to an education.

The example highlights two common beliefs about what advocacy means. Pat's mother and Principal Higgins believe they advocate what is fair to support and supervise the people they care for. In both cases, they choose to sacrifice the welfare of those they are not advocating for the benefit of their person(s). This is an example of advocacy without a balance of information and guiding principles of equity. Principal Higgins recognizes that Pat needs guidance and redirection. Pat's mother doesn't care about the teacher and other students' situation. Principal Higgins believes this is where the parent's support is essential for good behavior and an uninterrupted path to schooling. Pat's mother thinks it's her job to ensure Pat physically gets to school, and the rest is on the school system. Principal Higgins knows how Pat's mother feels but has nothing at his disposal to fix the immediate and long-term structural problem.

Both Pat's mom and Principal Higgins are great examples of the 6 and 18 silos that parents and schools operate day to day and year to year. The lack of Pat's mother realizing the critical role the parents play in teaching their child how to be successful in taking advantage of opportunities and Principal Higgins's understanding that parents lack action. Yet, the foundation of the dilemma is the school cannot do anything systematically to improve the situation. The path to recovery (tell me if this sounds familiar!) accepts that this is the core issue. There is no blame here, and there cannot be if we are to address the issue. Too often, we hear the phrase or something akin to "...well, they ought to know..." The immediate question is always, "Why is that?" Or "how would they know." The answer is clear: they don't know and cannot know that they don't know.

We need a clear understanding of the information, guidance, and opportunities we need to advocate to help parents be critical partners in our school communities. To be the fairest, we can be with parents, we need to support and educate them on their role as the primary teachers of students. Our ultimate goal of preparing students must first ensure our parents are ready to be the primary teachers of their students.

How to Break Down Barriers to Engagement

If you conduct an internet search and put in the inquiry box "minority parents do not trust schools," you will find a whole host of articles and entries that promote the idea that parent involvement in schools is lacking (and, in most cases, it is). Further, you will find ideas that schools have by design and de facto-created "cultural mismatches" and the cure is to have more parent and school partnerships. None of this information is wrong, nor is it misguided. Our curriculum needs more parental collaboration, cultural responsiveness, and celebration. The danger is that the solution is simply adding parents' cultural education modifications, and presto, everything now works. The result is a modification to an existing system that is not designed to work this way, and it provides no sustainable pathway to grow, develop, and change as needed.

Breaking down the barriers to engagement means understanding that it is all about relationships for the common purpose of the student's future. Since schools do not produce "widgets," we are not manufacturers but in the ultimate service industry. Therefore, our approach must change from the inside, student out, parents, and community to the outside in. Relationship growth is founded on the collective belief of a common idea. Our view is that the parent is the primary teacher of our students. Our common goal is for the students to have an equal chance at contributing to our society through the advancement of their dreams. Think of schools as the pathway to dreams of opportunity. Dreaming starts at home, and the foundation is solidified and supported throughout those 18 hours, summer, and other vacations.

The school's primary customers are the students, and we cannot serve the students if we knowingly do not help them be in their best position for success. To break down the barriers to relationships, schools need to focus on the student, listen to what the parent wants for their child, and work with the parent to support their needs.

Honoring the "C": Call, Contact, Coordination, Collaboration (Denise 1999)

Engagement is Education—Involvement is Compliance. Fair or not, the connotation of compliance is the passive-aggressive badge of courage. As a historian, I find it extraordinary that today's "soundbite" education policy-making of "school choice," prescription education evaluation, and education standards instead of curriculums are all hailed on the premise of not micromanaging and offering the most freedoms of executing the policies. Further, you will hear that the "built-in" competition structure will improve everyone. How is this idea an advancement on "separate but equal?" Education and its benefits are a process, and when the process is reduced to outcome compliances, the focus becomes the compliances, not the process. The underpinning belief has a complete disregard for our relative socio-economic positions in life due to financial security, race, social connections, and the interdependent nature of these realities; it adds up to our "privilege" in communities. Without accepting the interdependent nature of these facts, it is easier to understand the lack of buying into our collective responsibilities to one another. This is how we developed our education system, which suffers from structural inequities.

Administrators, teachers, and all involved in our schools can begin our relationship building by honoring the "C": *Call, Contact, Coordination, Collaboration.* Only through our persistent and honest dedication to bridging, developing relationships, and educating our parents can we lay the foundation for a system where parents who have fully informed partners in the dreams of their students can have an equitable opportunity education system.

Call: setting out the clear purpose of the parent partnership—to educate what it is to be the parent of a student and its responsibilities and the school's role to assist, educate, and foster connections.

Contact: the active pursuit of awareness, support, and the human element of connection. This is the process of "putting a face" on the school. Having a point person to guide, interpret, and counsel.

Coordination: bringing together community groups with the belief that parents are students' primary teachers. Our collective aim is to support their dreams for their child. This is the structural element of "putting the pieces together" for easier access and effect.

Collaboration: The final product and constant review of the system and structure developed and constantly refined its approaches and assumptions based on being true to its original intention of a more equitable school experience for the students.

Just Focusing on the Student Without the Parent Connection Is Just Short-Sighted and Selfish

Too often, exhausted, we accept educating in a vacuum of teachers and our students. It is confusing, for sure, but understandable. How often do we feel and express the frustration of not being supported at home by parents? Weird things happen as a result. As students move from the early elementary grades, we wear out trying to connect parents to their students' school life. Many parents have told me that getting some teachers and schools to post short-term and long-term assignments becomes a quest for the Holy Grail. To clarify, when I use the word "post," I talk about various communication options, from snail mailing home notices, posting on a class website, sending a pre-recorded phone message, text message, social site postings, or even podcasts. Posting assignments is far below the bare minimum, yet many parents do not have access to that information; it begs the question, what is the big secret?

Suppose parents have access to the curriculum combined in a real human-connected way. In that case, the teachers and school will increase their likelihood of parent support and lay the groundwork for a partnership. Much of the acrimony that is playing out at Board of Education meetings throughout the nation is a result of institutional ignorance. Schools do not openly leverage parents as the primary teachers of students. The parents do not understand their role as the primary teacher, so the absence of any real sense of what is going on in the classroom and how the parents, teachers, students, and school are to engage one another is the root of the consternation most of the time:

> The evidence is now beyond dispute. When schools work together with families to support learning, children tend to succeed not just in school but throughout life.
> (Henderson and Berla 1994)

Parents are tasked by circumstance to be a student's dream coordinator; schools provide the corridors to those opportunities. Bringing together the two primary influencers in a student's life is a powerful vehicle in our society. This is affecting the heart of equity in education.

Revisit the Child Study Team

Response to intervention programs is present today in many schools as a reaction to the recent standardized testing push throughout our country in an attempt to standardize a curriculum for all students regardless of their circumstances and drive instruction to that end:

> RtI focuses on the early prevention of academic difficulty, particularly in the areas of reading and math by: ensuring appropriate instruction for all students; monitoring students' progress; and. providing additional levels of

instructional assistance (intervention) for students who require support.

(NYSED 2013)

This is a mechanical solution to fixing the academic performances of students. Seeing students as individuals is commendable. However, this approach has often become a triage activity rather than a system to address the underlying issues many students face to perform well academically.

Some schools, recognizing that they had to go beyond the prescriptive pretest, monitor, and insert interventions, then re-test cycle, have chosen to form Child Study Teams. CST still concentrates on academic performance but also emphasizes discussion of the students, their circumstances, and a more holistic approach to interventions. Discussions of students who may be performing adequately but seem off or distracted are included, as are those who give other subtle signals that all may not be ideal in their lives. Those CSTs that are successful advocate for more actions, parent connections, and services available in the community for the families to become directly more involved in the student's academic life.

Connecting, supporting, and coordinating a student's education with their parents as active teachers and permitting them to guide their student outward from the inside of school is a huge jump for many. Parents are positioned to be change-makers for their students through a systematic approach that goes hand in hand with our schools. If schools coordinate the parents, education process, and community resources, we can solve community-based challenges and create sustainable environments for expanding opportunities for the youth of our society.

How to Employ Situational Leadership to Manage Your Vision

The construction of plans and ideas in a vacuum is one thing, but leading a vision and ensuring that all you do will ultimately lead to success is the devil in the details for any leader. In the late 1960s, Paul Hersey and Ken Blanchard introduced and developed the idea of "Situational Leadership" (Hersey and Blanchard, 1969). Throughout my years of education and leadership, I have found their approach to be the most powerful foundation for any leader's actions to accomplish tasks with a group of people. In a real sense, it is the foundation of collaboration.

When Hersey and Blanchard introduced the idea of SL, it was before the idea of separating the ideas of management and leadership. In other words, Hersey and Blanchard were not influenced to view one as a separate endeavor from the other as we are likely to do today. Many of today's studies of leadership primarily focus on the vision and studies of the results of efforts of ideas implemented but not on the mechanics of actually managing the vision. SL solely looks at the mechanics of bringing a group of people together to accomplish a task(s).

At the heart of using SL is the ability to assess the competence and commitment levels of those you work with and match the appropriate leadership approach to elevate the group's abilities and accomplish the initial task and any related tasks moving forward.

Blanchard, K. (1997). Recognition and situational leadership II. *Emergency Librarian,* **24(4), 38–38.**

Four Development Level Characteristics:

- D1 = Low Competence/High Motivation: New to task or goal, inexperienced; eager to learn, willing to take direction; enthusiastic, excited, optimistic; confidence based on hopes and transferable skills, not reality
- D2 = Some Competence/Low Commitment: Has some knowledge and skills, not competent yet, frustrated; discouraged, overwhelmed, confused; developing and learning, needs reassurance that mistakes are part of the learning process; unreliable, inconsistent
- D3 = High Competence/Variable Commitment: Is generally self-directed but needs opportunities to test ideas with others; sometimes hesitant, unsure, tentative; not always confident, self-critical, may need help in looking at skills objectively; may be bored with goal or task; makes productive contributions
- D4 = High Competence/High Commitment: Recognized by others as an expert; consistently competent, justifiably

confident; trust own ability to work independently, self-assured; inspired, inspires others; proactive, may be asked to do too much

Four Leadership Styles:

S1 = Directing: Help others gain confidence; Recruit new members to a group or organization
   Needs: high directive behavior and low supportive behavior. They need a leader who tells them specifically what to do.
S2 = Coaching: Employees at this stage ask a lot of questions. There is a great deal of both one-way and two-way communication: Starting a new initiative: curricular, schedule, policy; "selling" on new or modified approach technology.
S3 = Supporting: Employees at this state no longer need to be told what to do, but the leader must still be involved. A leader is a member of the committee or group facilitating the flow of ideas and challenges, advisory team work, curricular committee work, professional development/professional learning planning, and Child Study Team—RtI.
S4 = Delegating: When the members have the ability and the confidence to do what is needed, they need little to no direction. Just simply assign them tasks and let them do their jobs. Operating established programming; professional learning communities enacting their developed programs—worked-based learning and advisory teams.

 **Actionable Ideas**

Advisory Committee Portal
Social-Professional Media Connection
Where could it be Housed:

- ♦ Class Website: this is not ideal but could make it easier for the teacher—it serves the teacher but not the real purpose

- Stand-alone Web Page: better but not one that is likely to get the most traffic

Application: easiest in terms of access—both mobile (cell) phone and Google World

Purpose:

Connect the advisory team to the program and the program to the team

Ideas of how it can be used:

- Access to curriculum
- Opportunity to comment on curriculum, student interns, ideas for program
- Communicate in the field and connect updates to trade/profession
- Data collection repository to make advisory team meetings more interactive
- Provide a collaborative platform directly with the field to review the curriculum
- Assist in connecting to other businesses and owners that may or may not be a member of the advisory team → WBL landing places
- Improve and customize the Employability Profile form for Vo-tech students
- Grow the "stable" of mentors for current and future students
- Develop post-completion work experience/opportunity e-bulletin board
- Recruit more substitute TAs, LTAs, and Teachers
- Assist with Chamber of Commerce/Community Activities
- Resource Center for further education opportunities
- Add professional articles
- Add professional resource links for all advisory teams, teachers, WBL leaders, students, and alumni of the program.

Examples of Collaborative Learning Platforms

TABLE 6.1 10 Collaborative Learning Platforms

App/Tool	Free or $
Google Docs/Classroom	Free
EdApp	Free for basic use Pay for premium
Slack	$
Makers empire	$
Minecraft-education edition	$
StoriumEDU	$
Spiral	$
Mural	Free for basic use Pay for premium
Padlet	Free for basic use Pay for premium

* This list is neither an endorsement nor comprehensive.

Rules for Teacher-Administrator-School Community Leadership
Believe in All the People You Work with and Tell Them

Being an administrator in a school system is the loneliest position in the district, but you are not an island, and to be successful, you cannot operate as one. The most loyal people you will ever have in your organization will be those you recommend for hire; they are, in fact, "your people." Thus, those your predecessor(s) hired, those faculty/staff members remain "their" people. And, to add another odd twist to this formula, those who sat on selection/interview committees who recommended you for hire believe you are "their" administrator.

Given this layered psychological "ownership," your task is surprisingly straightforward: recognize your faculty/staff's positive qualities and affirm to them that you appreciate them for those traits, and, just like students, be specific with your praise. It personalizes the message and makes it an individual affirmation. While the goal is not to "convert" those who are not your people, it will establish a necessary working relationship built on respect so that you can have the opportunity to lead effectively.

If It Is Important, Do It

If it is important in your life, do it; this extends beyond being an administrator. In our role as the school community leader, we are ordained by the position to safeguard and lead the larger issues while overseeing how that translates to the smaller ones. Issues face us everywhere. For some, it is safeguarding children who become pawns for political and family issues; for others, it is opioid addiction, mental health, or fighting the forces that want to privatize public education. Some issues are closer to home, a partner no longer happy in the community and living in a fishbowl, and the strain of dealing with an aging parent and their needs. The same rule applies: Do the important stuff; it does matter. It is hard to believe that you can be an effective leader if what is important to you is not attended to. Sadly, I have seen friends and colleagues put aside those things; eventually, it just eats them up.

Legacy Is Important

It takes someone with a very healthy ego and air of self-confidence (remember what I said about the double-edged sword these qualities are) to become or want to become an administrator. I do not know of a single person who became an educator who went into the profession to limit student opportunities. Every administrator should make it their personal and professional goal to create something that either stands the test of time or create a platform or opportunity that can be built upon for student opportunities and growth in their district.

Legacy is essential; concretely, it formalizes what drives our professional pursuits. In a very public way, it demonstrates that in our time as the district leader, we did not simply collect a paycheck and become the master of compliance. Think about the legacy you want to be known for; was it something that enabled children to strive for excellence, created a supportive environment for opportunities, or was it a monument to your ego? While the last reflection may seem harsh, it is worth using it as a check on your goals and actions. Simply stated, as a leader, you must lead to something. What will your something become?

Small Things Are Important, but So Are Big Things

I hate boxes. Those ideas people put forward to characterize things and people to assist them in making sense of the world. Maybe it is a form of oppositional defiance I have, but I have noticed that it is a trait of leadership to reject this classification route. It is possible to be a detail person and still have a healthy appreciation of the big picture.

Life as a leader is about seeking and maintaining balance. The skill lies in understanding the balance between the leaves and the forest.

Balancing family and friends with your profession as an administrator is the key to your foundation as a leader. The old phrase "family first" is a simple reminder that those relationships define the person we are and the leader we can become. When leaders are out of whack, they look at achievements earned and make those their defining features as though they forged the success.

Defining the big pictures and filling them in with the small details enriches everyone. It provides depth to the experiences and enriches all those involved, inspiring others to operate and share in the goals. Structure, safety, collaboration, celebration, and commitment all rolled into one. Now that is a deal!

Learning Is Crisis Management

I was very fortunate to have an administration team intact for seven years, and we did some amazing things for students, teachers, and our staff. Melinda McCool, Simon Williams, and I adopted Simon's mantra (paraphrasing): "It's not a crisis; it's an opportunity." The correlation is "never let a crisis go to waste." Learning is stress management. Without stress, there is no growth; with too much stress, there is breakdown. It is the balance that becomes the key.

Learning is crisis management. How you approach the situation will determine the long-term success or continued failure. Child Study Teams (CSTs) are one of the districts' most powerful activities, provided they still need to become compliance-orientated. The CST is to review student academic progress data and vet and recommend remediation, but more importantly, it is about talking about the individual student. My work as an administrator and leader in this area is to give permission. Give permission to our educators to try things, and do not be afraid that the approach is "different," or the solutions are a bit off the beaten path. As a leader, to treat everyone the same, we must treat them differently.

> **Reflection**
>
> 1. How do schools around you honor the "C"?
> 2. What is the purpose of your parent-teacher-student organization; does your school have such an organization?
> 3. Make a list of your school's parent involvement practices and label them "compliance" or "education."

References

Denise, Leo. (1999). *Collaboration vs. c-three (cooperation, coordination, and communication)*. INNOVATINGReprint.

Henderson, A. T., & Berla, N. (1994). A new generation of evidence: The family is critical to student achievement, National Committee for Citizens in Education, Washington, DC..

Hersey, P., & Blanchard, K. H. (1969). Life cycle theory of leadership. *Training & Development Journal*, 23(5), 26–34.

NYSED (2013). https://www.p12.nysed.gov/docs/ais-rti.html (Retrieved December 4, 2023).

7

The Lesson of the Pandemic Digital Equity

A Crisis Is the Mother of Reform

Pandemic News: "Remote learning presents unique challenges for special needs students and their parents"; "East St. Louis students lacking internet for remote learning"; "Do schools turn in parents whose children do not participate in remote learning?"; "Teachers Consider Quitting Due to Overwhelming Hours, Online Issues, Class Sizes."

This snapshot of headlines during the pandemic represents several issues that came to the forefront. We must be prepared to use digital tools for an engaging learning platform and need to prepare to transform our education system.

Currently, the discussion centers on keeping students in class physically, dropping statewide testing, and student behavior in classes being reported in some areas as bad. The landscape of these concerns raises interesting questions. Why is teaching remotely universally a bad option? What are the underlying conditions and reasons for this conclusion? Is it due to equipment, access, teacher preparation, parent preparation, student preparation, or simply "e" all of the above? How do we "know" gaps in the student acquisition of knowledge? Is state-mandated testing purely reflective of a specific approach to learning? If we do not test, how do we know there are gaps? Is it essential to measure how we currently approach testing? Has it improved anything? Ok, THAT is a loaded question? Is current student behavior a reflection of worn-out teachers and administrators? Or is it simply students out of practice?

The challenge is on multiple equity fronts: a deficit in teacher training/preparation, digital instructional leadership, parents as digital teachers, and access/equipment.

My First Trip to the School Library

I remember the sense of the importance of going to the school library of my elementary school for the first time. We would learn how to unlock the card catalog and the mysteries of the Dewey Decimal System. With this knowledge, we leveraged the world's knowledge contained in all those books on the shelf. It was a huge day, yet I still do not remember my teachers doing much with the librarian to build it into what we did in the classroom. There was the occasional project, and we would "see the librarian" if we needed help, and the librarian, being only one person, really could not give us the time we needed. Another vivid memory is when my father bought the Funk and Wagnalls Encyclopedia set; he said we could look up anything alphabetically! So, I started getting information, copying verbatim for reports, and getting into trouble at school for the work not being my own. To add insult to injury, our teachers claimed that encyclopedias were not the best source of material and should have addressed the citations at the end of the articles, which could offer an avenue for information. Again, another potential path is blocked. It also boxed out my father from his approach to helping us. Instead of empowering the resources at hand, we were entirely dependent upon teachers. I am sure no one planned this or was even aware, but in the final analysis, it made no sense.

Today, our students have the world's knowledge in real time with 24-hour access in the palm of their hands every day. Ignoring this fact and not respecting its potential and necessity creates the damning problem that Alan November calls the "thousand dollar pencil." The resources available are flatting opportunities everywhere (Freidman 2005), and those who take advantage of them go to the front line. I would tell them the simple formula every year at my first meeting with my cross-country teams before the summer break. The best teams recognize that it is a team sport, not an individual one, and those teams who used each other to train daily were stronger and more innovative.

Coaching IS teaching. In this web 2.0 world and beyond, great classrooms recognize that individual achievements result from the collective resources used and shared for growth. To summarize, to be a great team, each has to be completely selfish (to be the best they can be) and selfless for the collective benefit of everyone.

The resources are here; it is now a matter of determining our purpose and leveraging our best resources to make it happen. Moving from a paradigm that the teacher is the center of the stage to an engagement facilitator takes work. Leaders must permit their teachers and staff to be leaders and explore possibilities with their students. The approach does not go against higher standards but enhances those goals. Lastly, we need to remember it STILL is about excellent teaching.

Should we teach information that can be "googled," or do we teach how to Google more accurately and effectively with an eye to ethical practices? Of course, we should be doing it; it only makes sense. Start the conversation and follow with action and support—nothing new here.

What about AI and the fear it is ruining everything and that all we care about in education and learning is now doomed? That was a bit dramatic, but those fears are rampant if you listen to conversations. Again, it comes down to good teaching, engagement, and learning trumps all.

Foundation of the "Digital Divide"
The cause of the digital divide is not new. Still, due to its exponential impact, it could become either its greatest leveler or divider of equity in our education system. Historians teach context is everything. Looking at something or a problem in isolation is

naive and dangerous to understand a situation. Root causes often result from actions taken not by design to harm others but from a lack of understanding of anything not within their experiences. Teachers had to teach "remotely" due to the lockdowns. Many attempted to recreate their daily activities in their classrooms on a vastly different platform. Without adequate background or ability to prepare to such a degree, synchronistic classes became the only option for most teachers, parents, and students—attendance by video presence and not necessarily engagement.

Our public school system is based on middle and upper-middle-class values of assumed support, availability, and vision for what and how students are educated. In *Brown v. The Board of Education of Topeka, Kansas*, the decision to end education segregation and the idea of "separate but equal" were labeled as inherently not equal. Due to economic opportunities, housing affordability, and migration patterns, we have re-established the idea of separate but equal. Our poorer communities, especially in urban areas, are over-represented by black and brown families. Additionally, due to our middle and upper-middle-class values, these families find themselves in structurally inadequate schools to affect positive upper mobility on a large scale. The pro-choice movement clamors as the answer, but it is not. Simply randomly picking students or using a selection process still does not affect the parenting deficit skills needed to support a vision of opportunity for the student. This solution applies to the 1960s–1970s attempts at bussing students to achieve integration. While this may sound harsh, the reality is many students fail prefabricated standards that are report cards of assumed growth in a vacuum.

The digital divide exists throughout our society, which is an odd way to make it more suitable to assist our community on all levels. The key to our (read: schools) efforts is on parental education, to focus on developing as digital citizens and consumers of information rather than on how to monitor specific applications a teacher may choose to use.

The Need for a Digital Skills Curriculum

The reform movement of the last 15 years has focused on designing new "standards of the curriculum." In the name of giving "curricular flexibility" on the ground, it has unleashed a bizarre game of playing to discover what the actual curriculum should be based on the accountability exams rather than just finishing the job of creating a curriculum. The effect is to force schools to align resources for this "discovery" of the curriculum and then write it. While schools in wealthy communities absorb the cost of personnel, time, and expert review more easily, it merely drains down resources in poorer neighborhoods. It adds another hurdle to the teachers teaching the curriculum and preparing its students and parents.

The primary focus of adult education efforts for parents is to guide and teach digital literacy. In the words of Alan November, "In a world of information overload, it is vital for students *and parents* to be able to find information on the Web, as well as to determine its validity and appropriateness." Empowering parents by educating them in basic digital literacy is the vehicle to connect the spaces between the known and unknown and provide opportunities to seek out possibilities beyond the physical confines of current situations. School parents are structurally equipped with these rudimentary digital skills; they are best situated in their educational role to assist their students.

Start with the simple premise of almost every school's mission statement; "Create Life-Long Learners." **Goal:** Develop students to be the best researchers they can be. The role of the teachers and parents becomes singularly aimed at facilitating this goal, teaching and reinforcing the skill sets needed to nurture the natural curiosity and need for ownership of their learning and, in essence, become "life-long learners."

So, what about the skills that are needed? Since the digital researching tools transcend all the subject areas of current schooling, they need integration K-12+, not assigned as a stand-alone. The best way is to develop a K-12 set of competencies considering the student's age and physical abilities.

Digital Fluency

Unlike the more traditional approaches to fluency, being able to express oneself easily and articulately, digital fluency brings an idiomatic element to the understanding. The digital dynamic is the attempt to underscore the engagement level of computer technology at the heart of the best of what the footprint offers and its most significant shortcomings.

Caveat Emptor, "let the buyer beware," is often understood to be the cautionary warning to ordinary consumers that products or services they may choose are fraught with signs that they may or may not easily understand or can research. While the context of the marketplace location of the products or service is enough of an accepted condition that can effectively give cautionary warnings, it often exploits the under-educated. The same is valid for engaging and consuming digital information.

Following up on the researcher's work at Stanford University Graduate School of Education in 2016, students needed help judging the credibility of information online:

> The report, released this week by the Stanford History Education Group (SHEG), shows a dismaying inability by students to reason about information they see on the Internet, the authors said. Essentially, the students lacked the ability to determine credible sources of information. Students, for example, had difficulty distinguishing advertisements from news articles or identifying where information came from (Donald, 2016).
> (https://ed.stanford.edu/news/stanford-researchers-find-students-have-trouble-judging-credibility-information-online -retrieved January 13, 2024)

In 2021, another report out of the Stanford University Graduate School of Education reported on a national study of high school students' digital skills. Again, significant difficulties were found for the students in vetting news stories and digital content.

The researchers suggested, "...potential remedies that might right the ship, including teaching students strategies based on what professional fact-checkers do--strategies that have been shown in experiments to improve students' digital savvy." (https://ed.stanford.edu/news/national-study-high-school-students-digital-skills-paints-worrying-portrait-stanford retrieved December 4, 2023).

The need for improvement is evident; the persistent gap in the abilities of both students and adults hampers many of our best efforts. This study aims to create the best supportive and collaborative environment for students using enhanced critical consuming and engaging researching skills to assist the parents at home with the same basic skills.

 **Actionable Ideas**

Sites:
From the Office of Educational Technology-Parent and Family Digital Learning Guide
Developing a Culture of Information Literacy: https://jcsonlineresources.org/wp-content/uploads/2019/12/Andrew-Stark_Developing.pdf (Retrieved January 13, 2024).

Ideas to Promote Digital Equity

One-to-One Device Programs: Implementing one-to-one device programs ensures that each student has access to a personal device, such as a laptop or tablet, fostering equal opportunities for digital learning.

Internet Accessibility Programs: Collaborate with local internet service providers to offer discounted or subsidized internet access to families with limited financial means. This ensures that all students can connect to online resources from home.

Digital Literacy Curriculum: Develop and integrate a comprehensive digital literacy curriculum to empower students with the skills needed to navigate and critically assess digital content, fostering a more inclusive learning environment.

Professional Development for Educators: Provide ongoing professional development opportunities for teachers to enhance their digital skills and incorporate technology effectively into their teaching methods, ensuring a consistent and high-quality digital learning experience for all students.

Equitable Distribution of Educational Technology: Ensure that the distribution of educational technology resources, such as software and learning apps, is equitable across all classrooms and grade levels, addressing potential disparities in access.

Collaboration with Community Organizations: Partner with local community organizations, businesses, and nonprofits to secure donations or sponsorships for digital devices and internet access, creating a support network for needy students.

Flexible Learning Environments: Implement flexible learning environments that accommodate various learning styles and preferences, allowing students to engage with digital content in ways that suit their needs.

Digital Inclusion Initiatives: Develop initiatives targeting underrepresented groups or marginalized communities, addressing unique challenges they may face regarding digital access and literacy.

Parental Engagement Programs: Create programs that involve parents in their children's digital education, providing resources and workshops to support families in navigating digital platforms and understanding the importance of digital literacy.

Monitoring and Evaluation: Regularly assess the impact of digital equity initiatives through data collection and analysis, adjusting strategies as needed to ensure ongoing effectiveness and address emerging challenges.

The next chapter is a sample of a K-12 Digital Citizenship & Competencies that I heavily borrowed and modified from Van Meter Community (Van Meter, Iowa) School Digital Citizenship & Digital Literature. This is an example, but it lays out the required skills and competencies, making it easier to identify and define what must be mastered. It takes the secrecy and mystery of the direction and purpose.

Rules for Pandemic-Digital Equity
STUDENTS AND SUPPORT STAFF MUST BE INCLUDED

The support staff are often left behind as an afterthought to the education system. A fatal mistake. It only runs smoothly in a school district with these individuals. They make the wheels turn, literally and figuratively. They are most likely school district residents and are de facto your most influential group within the community. They live and talk about school life in the local deli, in the market, and at the post office. Their view must include what everyone is doing. Otherwise, they cannot contribute positively.

Whatever way you choose to communicate digitally and collaborate, they need to use the same methods. When they suggest ideas and new ways to enhance how the school communicates, reaches out, and upgrades productivity in the digital world, work it through. A great way to empower them is to have them on the ground floor of your PD alongside your students, faculty, and staff. Then, encourage your secretaries and staff to lead their PD with other school district staff. Now, that is a digital collaboration to be reckoned with. Use the free video calling sources to make your contact with them more personal; it can lead to less miscommunication and understanding that often happen via emails and phone calls. Extend this idea that they should build a network of other professionals in surrounding and close school districts to troubleshoot situations and share insights.

A PHONE IS REALLY A COMPUTER

Quick, how many people do you know who do not have a cell/mobile phone? How many people do you know who no longer have a landline? Do you know how to make a phone call on a public phone? Can you find one? Just a few years ago, these seem like very strange questions. Despite this, many schools need help with their cell phone policies and trying to figure out how to get computers in the hands of all of our students. The answer to the latter situation is simple: They likely already have them. Today's cell phones are computers on which we occasionally make phone and video calls.

I have a cell phone that I do not have hooked up to a carrier. Because it has Wi-Fi, I can use it as a computer, and through Skype, Google Hangouts, FaceTime, and Facebook (along with many other options), I can call or video call for free. Many students and adults prefer using their cell devices as their computers. I witnessed this firsthand a couple of years ago, watching my daughter working on her Chromebook on an assignment when the battery died; she did not miss a beat. She picked up her cell phone and began typing. I was so inspired that at my next Commissioner Advisory Committee meeting, I challenged myself to use my cell phone to keep notes of the meeting and share them with my colleagues. Talk about empowering!

While using a cell phone may not be the most comfortable answer for school districts, it offers an interesting option to expand digital opportunities to many more students who may not have PCs or laptops at home for their exclusive use.

NEWSFLASH: PEOPLE LIKE THE FEELING OF BEING CONNECTED

I get such a kick out of people who lament how awful it is that our children are so addicted to their phones and, in the same breath, cannot wait to tell me the latest gossip from Facebook. The bottom line is that people like the connection to one another. For some, the attraction of the phone/computer is that they can answer on their terms and the relative space it provides (meaning the messages get there immediately whether you are feet or thousands of miles away).

We know that the immediacy of feedback is an absolute ingredient of student learning. In their hands, in our hands, are the tools to leverage that need and increase a student's world to being the world. I cannot imagine anything being more exciting, or for that matter, more natural for us.

IT'S ABOUT SOFT SKILLS

There is a push for career (and college, though it is all career) readiness, and people have become blinded by academic preparation in isolation. It is interesting to scan articles and blogs about the shortcomings of our new workers and their need for soft skills, not their academic training. Skills include leadership, relating professionally with each other, being able to produce, and being a collaborator. These traits employers value are the same ones we should value in an environment that places a premium on setting goals and celebrating achievement. School is the real world.

Soft skills are the human interaction element to how we carry on in life. In our pursuit of greater student engagement and collaboration, we need to guide our students in ethics and research to enable them to have greater and greater pathways of amazement. These lessons are beyond our computers and thousand-dollar pencils. The expectation, standard setting, and drive for resetting our collective social norms for each other have to include everything we do in and out of our classrooms.

BREAK THE BOUNDARIES OF YOUR BUILDING(S)

If there is one rule that sums up leading the digital charge, it is this one. The digital world builds on the shoulders of the traditional transcending device...books. While we only had our books to light imaginations in the past, we can now use books and articles from beyond our physical libraries and shelves worldwide. Our students, faculty, staff, and administrators can reach out and communicate, in real time, with the entire world. Have a discussion via the computer with an author, or teach another class in another school regardless of where in the world it is. Publish student work for the world to see and weigh in on.

As we challenge our students that the world is a much bigger place than their backyard, it is also that for you and me. Seek and enjoy the ride for everyone's future.

> **Reflection**
>
> 1. Define what you believe using technology means. Is your definition an input/output or interactive model involving collaboration? Does your definition involve or give instant feedback? How does your definition improve a student's skill, knowledge, or application? Does your definition create more work for a teacher?
> 2. Design a lesson that uses digital technology that contains all of the following in a school that has limited or inadequate funding: **Goal**: Discovery
>
> **Steps**: Application of new knowledge or skill, Reflection, and Articulation or Publishing.

Additional Resources

Blunt, T., & Magerko, B. (2019, February). Mapping the factors that impact technological fluency for black youth in low income communities. In 2019 Research on Equity and Sustained Participation in Engineering, Computing, and Technology (RESPECT) (pp. 1–2). IEEE.

November, A. (2012). *Who owns the learning? Preparing students for success in the digital age.* Solution Tree Press, Bloomington, Indiana.

References

Freidman, Thomas. (2005). *The world is flat.* New York: Farrar, Straus and Giroux 488.

https://ed.stanford.edu/news/national-study-high-school-students-digital-skills-paints-worrying-portrait-stanford (Retrieved December 4, 2023).

8

The Good Stuff

Interdependent Nature of Education

The excitement of putting together a program is the lack of boundaries you have in initially setting it up. The ideas I am putting forth are not intended to be written in stone; they are ideas to help you create a structure that works for you from the collective wisdom and resources of your community and school. Your program is designed to fit the needs of your families. Some elements go into this structure that I highly recommend. First, there is a total commitment to the base idea that you are combining forces to focus on the need to assist parents to be their students' best primary teachers. Second, there are multiple collaborative feedback loops to inform decisions, and all understand that this process is never "finished" in the sense it is a complete product. It needs to be approached as a living model that adjusts repeatedly as resources, needs, and aspirations dictate.

TABLE 8.1 Basic Engagement Program Elements

Element	Description	A basic list- MUST be adapted to fit your community needs!
Welcome Basket	The foundation of the Parent-to-School Community Program. A physical "welcome basket" that must have school shirts for parents and newborns in the school colors, name, and mascot: this is the physical "uniform" of belonging to the school community; there must be shirts for both parents and the newborn student.	• Contact Information: schools, pediatricians, clinics, family services, social security, churches, urban league, mental health outreach, day-care providers, and other family-orientated groups. • Developmental Charts & pamphlets • Medical recommendations for newborns & toddlers • Nutrition advice • Activities for parents & newborn • Mental Health recommendations for both parents & newborn • Timeline of important newborn development checkpoints • Immunization schedule • Safe Samples of anything & everything from diapers to formula • Digital Directory for any of the above information
Toddler Orientation	The In-person Welcome Basket is coming to life. This is where we begin building physical relationships with the parents as a school community. At the orientation, representatives from all the items are present to meet, greet, and expand upon everything in the basket, plus the PK & K teachers.	• Arrangements for transportation • Arrangements for childcare (think of using older students) • Multimedia campaign to get the word out • Send out personal invitations to parents- physical, **not digital** • Arrange for food- dinner and not just pizza • Make sure you have multi-linguistic assistance. MUST include your ELL/ENL faculty and staff

(Continued)

TABLE 8.1 (Continued)

Element	Description	A Basic List Must Be Adapted to Fit Your Community Needs!
Parent as Primary Teachers Curriculum	Based on the readiness to learn skill sets, development research, and the soft skills of executive function this is the keystone of the efforts of the school & community to "train" its parents in their role as the primary teacher of their students. Within this framework is raising opportunity awareness for their student's future & a pathway to achieving those dreams.	<ul><li>Broken down chronologically</li><li>Based on research child development</li><li>Based on readiness to learn skills development</li><li>Supporting materials to include but NOT limited to Adult Education, videos, pamphlets, arranged meetings with a counselor, and community groups, laptops, internet service</li><li>The input of PK & K teachers</li><li>Have multiple language versions as needed</li></ul>
Counselor/ Mentor	This is the central figure that is the physical connection between the parent and the school. Unlike the traditional school counselor, who primarily works with the student, this counselor/mentor's primary contact is with the pre-PK parent.	<ul><li>Make a connection with local colleges/universities teacher & counselor prep programs- this is an ideal pre-service experience for teachers & counselors in training</li><li>Register parents at Toddler Conference</li><li>Point person for P.I.E.P.; School-Community-Parent Study Team, Adult Education</li><li>Parent Inventory coordinator</li><li>Single source for parents to contact for all information about school & community agencies</li></ul>

(Continued)

TABLE 8.1 (Continued)

Element	Description	A Basic List Must Be Adapted to Fit Your Community Needs!
Parent-School-Community Study Team	Parallels existing school's child study teams. The focus of this group is to monitor the needs of our Pre-PK parents through in-person contact, P.I.E.P., and Parent-issued Report Cards of Students. Make recommendations to parents and actively assist in connecting parents to appropriate agencies if needed.	• Based on regularly scheduled contacts • Parent feedback • Coordinate the Parent-Issued Report Card to the assessments used in the Study Team • Plan of follow-up to be included in the P.I.E.P.
Adult Education	Supplemental learning and training opportunities that are informed from multiple sources: Counselors/Mentor; P.I.E.P.; Parent-School- Community Study Team; Parent-Issued Report Card.	• Prepare for multiple language support • Transportation Logistics • Child-care logistics • Include students in the learning and training opportunities • Multi-media publicity for these opportunities • Provide a collection of coordinated recorded sessions available to the public • offer both in-person and remote access- both synchronically and asynchronically

(Continued)

TABLE 8.1 (Continued)

Element	Description	A Basic List Must Be Adapted to Fit Your Community Needs!
Parent-Issued Student Report Card	Recognizing that the parent is the primary teacher of their child/student, the parent-issued report card provides the school with direct feedback from the teacher-parent. This progress monitoring of the student provides opportunities for connecting to needed assistance, support, and training to support the parent-teacher as she/he prepares their student.	• Use a chart to track the progress of skills • Do not use a rubric- it is a limiting device • Support artifact portfolio that will be shared and reviewed between parent and counselor • Develop an inventory needs assessment with the parent for both the parent's growth as the primary teacher & the student • Multi-language device
Semi-Annual PD/PL	Similar to Adult Education except that these professional development and learning opportunities include teachers, parents, and students.	• Developed from the direction of teachers, parents, & students • Focus is on the interdependency of the support at home and the activities that happen in the classrooms • Feedback from the Big Three Stakeholders: students, teachers, parents

(Continued)

TABLE 8.1 (Continued)

Element	Description	A Basic List Must Be Adapted to Fit Your Community Needs!
Extra-curricular Activities	Any program for students that occurs before or after school traditional hours. In their purest form, these activities serve as extensions to the curriculum of the school. Their purpose is to provide opportunities to expand & teach & reinforce practical application skills.	<ul><li>Coordinated with curriculum</li><li>Active conversations with parents, students, & classroom teachers</li><li>Collaborate with Community Agencies and leaders to leverage resources & opportunities</li><li>Establish clear competencies to be achieved in the programs</li><li>Transportation logistics</li><li>Childcare logistic coordination</li><li>Multiple-language access</li></ul>
Honoring the "C"	**Call:** setting out the clear purpose of the parent partnership **Contact:** the active pursuit of awareness, support, and the human element of connection. **Coordination:** bringing together community groups under a single common belief that parents are the primary teachers of students and our collective aim is to support their dreams for their child. **Collaboration:** the final product and constant review of the system and structure that is developed and constantly refining its approaches and assumptions based on being true to its original intention of a more equitable school experience for the students.	<ul><li>Multi-language assistance</li><li>Multimedia, Multi-Platform Public Relations</li><li>Gatherings that celebrate parents as teachers- make sure there is food! (More than pizza!)</li><li>Competency-based action PlansTo</li><li>Understand that structural feedback loops must be ongoing and adjusted as needed</li></ul>

Resources for Parents to Use in Charting Developmental Milestones for Children

Charts to Use for Monitoring Child Development Progress—Bases for Parent-Issued Report Cards

Typical and atypical childhood development module 1-Wisconsin Department of Health Services (.gov): https://www.dhs.wisconsin.gov/clts/waiver/county/mod1-matrices.pdf (Retrieved January 3, 2024)

Typical and atypical child development module 2-Wisconsin Department of Health Services (.gov): https://www.dhs.wisconsin.gov/clts/waiver/county/mod2-matrices.pdf (Retrieved January 3, 2024)

Charts and Discussion

Help me grow (MN) 5 year child development milestones: https://helpmegrowmn.org/HMG/DevelopMilestone/5Years/index.html (Retrieved January 3, 2024)

Cognitive and social skills to expect from 3 to 5 years—American Psychological Association: https://www.apa.org/act/resources/fact-sheets/development-5-years (Retrieved January 3, 2024)

Important milestones: Your baby by five years—Centers for Disease Control and Prevention (.gov): https://www.cdc.gov/ncbddd/actearly/milestones/milestones-5yr.html (Retrieved January 3, 2024)

Developmental milestones table-University of Washington: https://depts.washington.edu/dbpeds/Screening%20Tools/Devt%20Milestones%20Table%20%28B-6y%29%20PIR%20%28Jan2016%29.msg.pdf (Retrieved January 3, 2024)

TIMELINE OF KEY ACTIVITIES

The 6 and 18 balance is the structure of learning for every student in public education today; simply moving the time shift an hour one way or the other will not enhance the equity of opportunity in a significant manner. Parents and their role in a student's learning and opportunities need to be the focus of our attention. Below is a chart based on a student's chronological order for activities that are recommended for the systematic engagement and education of parents as the primary teachers of their students.

TABLE 8.2 Chart of Activities

When?	Primary Target	Element	Players	Chapter
Birth	Parent	Welcome to the World Basket	School & Community	4
Age 2-Graduation	Parent	Toddler Orientation	School & Community	4
Age 2-Graduation	Parent	Counselor or Mentor	Counselor or Mentor	4
Age 2-Graduation	Family	Parent-School-Community Study Team	Counselor, Community Reps, Parent, Student	4
Birth - Graduation	Parent	Re-Imagined Adult Education	School & Community	4
Age 2-6	Parent & Student	Parent Issued Report Card	Counselor or Mentor	4
Age 3-Graduation	Parent, Student, & Teachers	Semi-Annual PD/PL	Family, School, & Community	4
Age 5-Graduation	Students	Extracurricular Activities	School, Parents, Students, & Community	5
Birth-Graduation	Families	Honoring the "C"	Administrators & Teachers	6

Feedback Loops and Resource Articles

To support this design, accepting that it is an ever-evolving and supporting process is necessary. Structural feedback loops are a key conduit to this process, providing all stakeholders a clear path of decision-making and collaboration. The key persons in this process are the parents and the counselor.

The first feedback is the Welcome Basket and the Toddler Orientation. The orientation's basis is the basket's contents and the formal beginning of establishing human contact and relationships. At the Toddler Orientation, all representatives

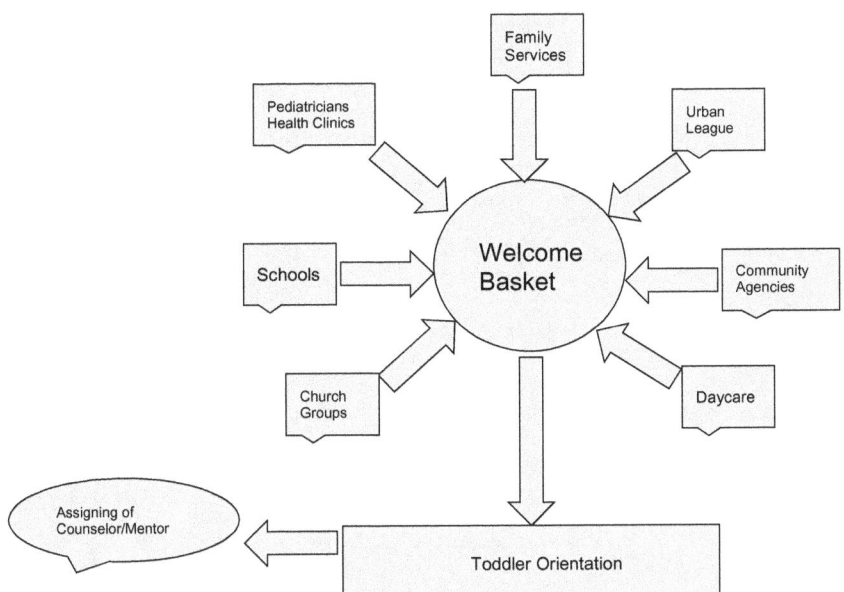

FIGURE 8.1 Welcome Basket and the Toddler Orientation

of the Welcome Basket are present to meet, greet, guide, and solidify contact. The assignment of the counselor/mentor will also happen at this meeting.

At the heart of the approach is improving the education process and the interdependent nature of the Parent-Student-School connection. It is a very personal relationship and of the utmost importance for the student's future; it must be honored in this way. The priority is establishing the trust and purpose of each other and the process.

Resources
Please note this is NOT an exhaustive list but a place to start
Articles:

Angelis, J. I., & Wilcox, K. C. (2011). Poverty, performance, and frog ponds: What best-practice research tells us about their connections. *Phi Delta Kappan*, 93(3), 26–31.

Bower, H. A., & Griffin, D. (2011). Can the Epstein model of parental involvement work in a high-minority, high-poverty elementary school? A case study. *Professional School Counseling*, 15(2), 2156759X1101500201.

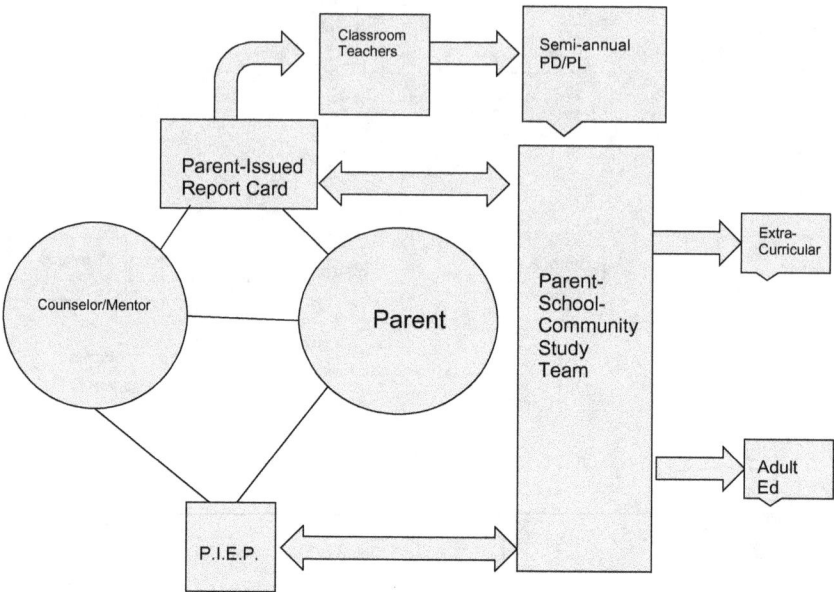

FIGURE 8.2 Parent-Student-School Connection

Watkins, C. S., & Howard, M. O. (2015). Educational success among elementary school children from low socioeconomic status families: A systematic review of research assessing parenting factors. *Journal of Children and Poverty*, 21(1), 17–46.

https://www.opencolleges.edu.au/informed/features/10-common-learning-myths-might-holding-back/ (Retrieved May 19, 2020).

https://www.occc.edu/support/characteristics.html (Retrieved January 6, 2021).

https://ny-kids.org/teacher-parent-interactions-distinguish-odds-beating-high-schools/ (Retrieved January 6, 2021).

PK-12 Digital Sample Curriculum-Students

The Covid-19 Pandemic brought to light a public education system that is unprepared to take on remote education in the form of a digital platform. Instead of advancing the transformation of learning, we scrambled to replicate an in-person experience on a platform that is not suited to such use. Worse still, our teachers and schools were not prepared for this immediate transition and could not lend support to the student's primary teachers, aka parents. To create a starting point of what students should know and when is a good time, I modified this work by the Van Meter Community School from Iowa and separated specific competency indicators that are outgrowths of the goals.

Case Study: Who Should Be in PD/PL

A few years ago, my wife, Laurie (teacher), myself, and our daughter, Molly, a senior in high school at the time, conducted a PD/PL for teachers and teaching assistants on how they could expand the use of their Google Classrooms to make them more engaging. Our first error was not getting involved in constructing the session groups. The district broke the groups into teachers and teaching assistants as separate entities. We immediately questioned the wisdom of that since the teaching assistants and the teachers work together in the classrooms, and it would be ideal to have them together to share ideas and synergy with their students. The response we received was that this is how they always did these things. However, a related but bigger lesson was about to happen.

Laurie and I presented and attempted to engage the group (we had the teaching assistants first), and they were politely asked a few questions between looking at their phones and the screens. When it was time for Molly to take over and share what she was doing in her school with Google Classroom, the place transformed. Phones disappeared, and without provocations, questions came from everywhere; they hung on her every word, engaged with every response, and just wanted more. Laurie and I just sat back, controlled the traffic, and offered sparingly when we could add something to the dynamic. It was easy to understand what was going on. Molly was the opportunity they had to pick the mind of a student, giving honest feedback on what engaged her as a student and what perceived positives and negatives came from past attempts from teachers and teaching assistants she had direct contact with. We think it also helped that she was not one of their students but still a student using the

TABLE 8.3 K-12 Digital Citizenship Competencies for New York State

Goal: Create Better Student Researchers

All Grades: K-12+ Digital Citizenship	All Grades: K-12+ Competency Indicators	K-12 Computer Science and Digital Fluency Learning Standards of New York State
• Critical Consumers of Digital Information • Use digital tools to advance their knowledge and provide a legacy of advancement	• Improve questioning skills: • Ask deeper questions	
Kindergarten: Digital Citizenship	**Kindergarten Competency Indicators**	Grades K-1 NYS Standards http://www.nysed.gov/common/nysed/files/programs/curriculum-instruction/computer-science-digital-fluency-standards-k-1.pdf
• States reasons why not to use first and last names when online • Asks for help at home and at school • Uses technology to explore personal interests • Uses technology responsibly explaining the difference between appropriate and inappropriate actions when using the internet and being online	• Improve questioning skills: • Ask deeper questions • Identifies the URL • Logs into computer and/or website • Uses a mouse/trackpad • Control the cursor on the screen by moving the mouse. • Click and drag to move objects on a screen • A single click and double click objects • Uses a tablet • Launches and quits programs • How to tell the difference between applications • Works independently on the computer or with a partner • Discusses appropriate and inappropriate ways to handle hardware and equipment	

Copyright material from Patrick Darfler-Sweeney (2025), *Fostering Parent Engagement for Equitable and Successful Schools: A Leader's Guide to Supporting Families and Students*, Routledge.

TABLE 8.3 (Continued)

Grade 1 Digital Citizenship	Grade 1 Competency Indicators	Grades K-1 NYS Standards http://www.nysed.gov/common/nysed/files/programs/curriculum-instruction/computer-science-digital-fluency-standards-k-1.pdf
• Explains why there are logins and passwords on some pieces of hardware, software, and websites • Generates safe usernames • Discusses the difference between personal and private information • Explains the difference between appropriate and inappropriate actions when using the internet and being online • Asks peers for help • Uses technology to explore personal interests • Demonstrates to others how to use technology tools in ways that assist, rather than prevent, others from learning	• Improve questioning skills: • Ask deeper questions • Identifies different types of domain names (.com, .org, .gov, etc.) • Mousing • Basic search process • Video/Video Cast • Podcasting • Uses basic output devices (headphones, speakers, etc.) • Explains how to clean screens appropriately • Utilizes word processing application to share original writing • Saves work to a specified location before closing applications • Students will be able to explore a program they have not used before without being given instructions	

(Continued)

TABLE 8.3 (Continued)

Grade 2 Digital Citizenship	Grade 2 Competency Indicators	Grades 2–3 NYS Standards http://www.nysed.gov/common/nysed/files/programs/curriculum-instruction/computer-science-digital-fluency-standards-2-3.pdf
• Describes why stealing information and things others have created is the same as stealing tangible items • Identifies ways to protect identity when contributing information online • Identifies examples of concerns that should go to an adult right away • Uses technology to explore personal interests • Demonstrates to others how to use technology tools in ways that assist, rather than prevent, others from learning • Uses information gained from the illustrations and words in a print or digital text to demonstrate understanding (fiction and nonfiction) • Compares and contrasts two or more versions of the same story (e.g. Fairy Tales, Night Before Christmas around World) by different authors or from different cultures.	• Improve questioning skills: • Ask deeper questions • Uses basic input and output devices (cd-ROM, flash drive, printer, microphones, etc.) • Tutorials • Video/Video Casting • Recognizes when an application or device is not working properly • Relaunches application as a troubleshooting measures • Utilizes presentation application and Web 2.0 tools to share information	

(Continued)

TABLE 8.3 (Continued)

Grade 3 Digital Citizenship	Grade 3 Competency Indicators	Grades 2–3 NYS Standards http://www.nysed.gov/common/nysed/files/programs/curriculum-instruction/computer-science-digital-fluency-standards-2-3.pdf

• Describes copyright
• Explains ways identity is protected when contributing information online
• Discusses what information is appropriate to share about other people (images, video, audio, text, etc)
• Considers personal information a stranger could find online
• Uses appropriate posture while working at a computer to avoid injury
• Uses technology to explore and pursue personal interests
• Shows others how to use new technologies, and use technology in ways that assist, rather than prevent, others from learning
• Using AI appropriately
	• Improve questioning skills:
	  • Ask deeper questions
	  • Basic typing class
	• Recognizes menu bars for basic applications (word processing, browser windows)
	• Uses word processing skills to manipulate and change the text
	• Begin using search file extensions
	• Uses technology tools to capture images (video and photos)–makes a lesson tutorial
	• Creates a multimedia presentation (Powerpoint, Keynote)
	• Connects hardware for multimedia presentation
	• Uses an external device to save and transfer files
	• Keys home row accurately and confidently
	• Student develops well-constructed questions, or line of inquiry that leads to better results from AI and Google searches for information	

(Continued)

TABLE 8.3 (Continued)

Grade 4 Digital Citizenship	Grade 4 Competency Indicators	Grades 4–6 NYS Standards http://www.nysed.gov/common/nysed/files/programs/curriculum-instruction/computer-science-digital-fluency-standards-4-6.pdf
<ul><li>Gives credit to the owner of visual media</li><li>Protect other people's personal information when publishing online (images, video, audio, text, etc)</li><li>Explain ways to tell if a stranger is using Internet information to seem like a friend</li><li>Describe consequences when people do not protect personal information when using social networking tools</li><li>Use technology responsibly to explore and pursue personal interests</li><li>Show others how to use new technologies, and use technology in ways that assist, rather than prevent, others from learning</li><li>Critically investigate internet generated information</li></ul>	<ul><li>Improve questioning skills:<ul><li>Ask deeper questions</li></ul></li><li>Identify the positive value of technology including web 2.0 tools</li><li>Advanced searching- checking the validity of sites</li><li>Use search operators</li><li>Use of "way back machine"</li><li>Using state and international codes in searches</li><li>Blogging</li><li>Website Creations</li><li>Publishing for a wider audience</li><li>Uses visual space on the desktop to display two programs at once</li><li>Utilizes spreadsheet and Web 2.0 tools to demonstrate numerical information</li><li>Creates a multimedia presentation by choosing from applications and Web 2.0 tools</li><li>Creates hyperlinks</li><li>Keys alphabet accurately and confidently</li><li>Serves as Class Scribe</li><li>Critically police information produced on the internet- better digital consumer</li></ul>	

(Continued)

TABLE 8.3 (Continued)

Grade 5 Digital Citizenship	Grade 5 Competency Indicators	Grades 4–6 NYS Standards http://www.nysed.gov/common/ nysed/files/programs/curriculum- instruction/computer-science- digital-fluency-standards-4-6.pdf
• Debate benefits and safety concerns of contributing information online • Recognize digital resources that are copyright free • Credits author and publication for direct quotations • Use technology responsibly to explore and pursue personal interests • Show others how to use new technologies, and use technology in ways that assist, rather than prevent, others from learning • Describe how communication changes online versus face-to-face • Deeper digital researcher skill sets	• Improve questioning skills: • Ask deeper questions • Join Media Minions(AV Squad) after passing Google certification courses • Publishing for a wider audience • Who owns the site & what does that mean? • Suggest a technology tool to use to accomplish a particular task • Utilizes spreadsheet and web 2.0 tools to organize, graph, and calculate data • Apply advanced formatting techniques • Sequence animation to produce a digital story • Keys letters and numbers at a productive speed • Explores tools to help with personal learning styles (organization tools like stickies and calendars, speech features from the text, highlighting, bookmarking tools) year prior to 1:1 computing • Develop a multiple modalities chapter / unit review lesson • Develop digital research flow charts	

(Continued)

TABLE 8.3 (Continued)

Grades 6–8 *Asterisk indicated skills taught in 6th-grade technology class**	Grade 6–8 Competency Indicators	Grades 4–6 NYS Standards http://www.nysed.gov/common/nysed/files/programs/curriculum-instruction/computer-science-digital-fluency-standards-4-6.pdf Grades 7–8 NYS Standards http://www.nysed.gov/common/nysed/files/programs/curriculum-instruction/computer-science-digital-fluency-standards-7-8.pdf
Digital Citizenship • Recognizes copyright law* • Uses citation tools* • Identifies consequences of plagiarism in school and beyond* • Identifies fair use* • Choose settings in account profiles that protect personal information when online* • Uses etiquette considering global audience when communicating digitally.* • Describes the concept of a digital footprint* • Interact and collaborate with peers, experts, and others using technology* • Debate legal and ethical uses of file sharing • Discuss the effects of existing and emerging technology on the global community • Analyze how cultures and groups value technology differently and how these values influence the development and acceptance of technology	• Improve questioning skills: • Ask deeper questions • **Media Minions deployed throughout the school to assist in PD, and classrooms** • Uses quick-fix tips to troubleshoot basic computer errors* • Explore tools to help with personal learning styles (organization tools like stickies and calendars, speech features for text, highlighting, etc)* • Use online collaboration tools to complete a task* • Use collaborative electronic communications to explore, share, and publish with other learners around the world* • Describe digital tools that help connect with personal interests*Personalize screen real estate for productivity and efficiency* • Keys with effective rate and accuracy to capture a free flow of thoughts* • Defends against SPAM, Phishing, and other digital scams/solicitations in email and other social media* • Demonstrate ability to use AI ethically for all competencies listed	

Copyright material from Patrick Darfler-Sweeney (2025), *Fostering Parent Engagement for Equitable and Successful Schools: A Leader's Guide to Supporting Families and Students*, Routledge.

TABLE 8.3 (Continued)

Grades 9–12 Digital Citizenship	Grade 9–12 Competency Indicators	Grades 9–12 NYS Standards http://www.nysed.gov/common/nysed/files/programs/curriculum-instruction/computer-science-digital-fluency-standards-9-12.pdf
• Use digital media and environments to communicate and work collaboratively, including at a distance, to support individual learning and contribute to the learning of others • Explain the impact of digital footprint on both personal and professional settings • Identify the intellectual property rights of personal content • Identify primary, secondary sources of information • Identify the methods used to influence a digital audience and how to gard against the various practices	• Improve questioning skills: • Ask deeper questions • Chooses technology tools to create digital content for information and/or expression • Apply digital tools to gather, evaluate, and use information • Utilize a working knowledge of technology or technology support services to identify problems/issue and its solution • Develop an interactive product to serve as a capstone project • Develop a process to identify information that is presented to primarily influence with dubious claims and information	

* Adapted from Van Meter Community School Digital Citizenship & Digital Literature.

same platforms and could speak to those experiences without prejudice from being one of their classroom students. For the afternoon session with the teachers, Laurie and 1 drastically reduced our direct involvement and conveyed the information from the perspective of Molly, the student. The result was one of the best sessions we have ever conducted. We did the same presentation again in a different school district during the spring semester with the same enthusiastic result.

The message is simple: if the purpose of the session is to increase student engagement, then it is a great idea to test and get the reaction from the people you are trying to assist.

Resources:
Please note this is NOT an exhaustive list but a place to start
State of Our Web Literacy Today: Donald, B. (2016). *Stanford researchers find students have trouble judging the credibility of information online.* News Center.

https://hosted.learnquebec.ca/nextschool/wp-content/uploads/sites/23/2018/08/Stanfordresearchersfindstudentshavetroublejudgingthecredibilityofinformationonline.pdf (Retrieved December 28, 2021).

An excellent starting point for Web Literacy Ideas: https://novemberlearning.com/educational-resources-for-educators/web-literacy/

Companion Books of Ideas: November, A. (2012). *Who owns the learning? Preparing students for success in the digital age.* Solution Tree Press: Bloomington, Indiana.

Web Literacy:
Kuiper, E., Volman, M., & Terwel, J. (2009). Developing web literacy in collaborative inquiry activities. *Computers & Education, 52*(3), 668–680.

Parry, D. (2011). Mobile perspectives: On teaching mobile literacy. *Educause Review, 46*(2), 14–16.

Article/Discussion
https://internethealthreport.org/v01/web-literacy/ (Retrieved January 6, 2021).

https://www.educatorstechnology.com/2016/07/some-helpful-activities-and-resources.html

PK-12 Digital Sample Competency-Based Skills for Parents in Supporting Their Students

This competency-based support chart could be used in conjunction with the P.I.E.P. and the reimagined Adult Education ideas that are explored in Chapter 4: Educate the Parents. The Competency Indicators are designed to support the previous student chart but are easily modified to fit most school's digital competency indicators.

TABLE 8.4 PK-12 Digital Sample Competency-Based Skills

Birth-Age 6-What parents need to support their student's education:	Birth-Age 6 Competency Indicators for Parents
Curiosity Information Literacy Love of Reading	• Conduct basic Google Search • Uses Search Operators • Uses country codes • Can distinguish advertisement from factual claims • Can Perform basic functions of email; attaching files; saving files • Can video and upload • Can schedule and host a Google Meet, Zoom, and Skype Video Meeting • Can use Google Translate
Age 7-Age 10-What parents need to support their student's education: Curiosity Digital Responsibility- Good Digital Citizenship Love of Reading Own their Learning Write/Publish for a World-Wide Audience Collaborate with others on a project/product Wellness Develop a Tutorial	Age 7–Age 10 Competency indicators for parents • Can identify the primary source from the secondary source material • Can develop and manipulate a spreadsheet • Can use parental digital controls • Knows all of their student's passwords • Can develop a multimedia presentation using more than one platform with their student

(Continued)

Copyright material from Patrick Darfler-Sweeney (2025), *Fostering Parent Engagement for Equitable and Successful Schools: A Leader's Guide to Supporting Families and Students*, Routledge.

TABLE 8.4 (Continued)

Age 11-14- What parents need to support their student's education:	Age 11-Age 14 Competency Indicators for Parents
Curiosity Digital Responsibility & Citizenship Love of Reading Own their Learning Write/Publish for a World-Wide Audience Collaborate with others on a project/product Wellness Develop a Tutorial for each subject Career Exploration and Goals	• Can develop a multimedia portfolio • Can formulate research questions • Can conduct a Google Scholar Search • Can use parental digital controls to track student's use and devices
Age 14-Graduation- What parents need to support their student's education:	Age 14-Graduation Competency Indicators for Parents
Curiosity Digital Responsibility & Citizenship Love of Reading Own their Learning Write/Publish for a World-Wide Audience Develop a Tutorial for each subject and unit Career Exploration and Goals Develop a Capstone Project (a.ka. Legacy Project) Personal Plan for Grades 9-12 Personal Plan for 4 years beyond HS Graduation	• Can digitally produce their story and legacy to share with their student

Resources

Please note this is NOT an exhaustive list but a place to start

Multi-layered resource about how to Google Search from Google: https://support.google.com/websearch/answer/134479?hl=en

Search operator list: https://ahrefs.com/blog/google-advanced-search-operators/

Internet country domains list (TLDs): https://www.worldstandards.eu/other/tlds/

USA state abbreviation list used for web searches: https://www.50states.com/abbreviations.htm

Educational Handouts & Lesson Plan Tips: https://novemberlearning.com/educational-resources-for-educators/educational-handouts-lesson-plan-tips/

Reflection

1. Identify areas of need to accomplish the competency indicators. Label the needs as Professional Development/Learning, Equipment, or Access.
2. Create the list of what your school is doing using this chart form and compare it to this chart.
3. Are students a part of your digital workshops for Teachers, LTA, and TA to get insights into their perspectives?

Additional Resources

Angelis, J. I., & Wilcox, K. C. (2011). Poverty, performance, and frog ponds: What best-practice research tells us about their connections. *Phi Delta Kappan*, *93*(3), 26–31.

Bower, H. A., & Griffin, D. (2011). Can the Epstein model of parental involvement work in a high-minority, high-poverty elementary school? A case study. *Professional School Counseling*, *15*(2), 2156759X1101500201.

Kuiper, E., Volman, M., & Terwel, J. (2009). Developing web literacy in collaborative inquiry activities. *Computers & Education*, *52*(3), 668–680.

National Research Council. (2015). *Transforming the workforce for children birth through age 8: A unifying foundation.*

Parry, D. (2011). Mobile perspectives: On teaching mobile literacy. *Educause Review*, *46*(2), 14–16.

Watkins, C. S., & Howard, M. O. (2015). Educational success among elementary school children from low socioeconomic status families: A systematic review of research assessing parenting factors. *Journal of Children and Poverty, 21*(1), 17–46.

https://www.opencolleges.edu.au/informed/features/10-common-learning-myths-might-holding-back/ (Retrieved May 19, 2020).

https://www.occc.edu/support/characteristics.html

https://ny-kids.org/teacher-parent-interactions-distinguish-odds-beating-high-schools/ (Retrieved January 6, 2021).

9
Final Thoughts

Dreaming

Dreamer was a label that my parents gave me. It was not a compliment. Oddly, it served me well, though the intention was not to do so; giving me the space to explore in my head and role-play ideas and situations became a powerful avenue for me to make decisions and fully inform myself. My parents helped create the dreamer in me by fueling the flames of curiosity and exploration. Dreaming was the process I internally developed to process that fuel.

We build on the experiences we encounter in life and attach applications for problem-solving and action to fit our talents, needs, and desires. The extension of this thinking is the more opportunities we have, the more options we have to use this cycle. It is not unlike the reasons we design curriculum to have students read more and varied types of literature and research that progressively gets more intricate to fill up their reservoir of ideas, vocabulary, and experiences that go beyond the boundaries of the physical spaces of the classroom. If you think about that last idea, you can start to understand the reasons for excitement in integrating digital tools to enhance experiences that further break physical limitations and can enhance deeper interactions on multiple dimensions.

Context: Going Backward to Go Forward

In 1440, Johannes Gutenberg's movable type invention singularly developed the pathway to inform and educate the masses. It was driving down the cost of reproducing classic works and new ideas, allowing these new and older inspirations into the hands of a much wider audience.

The old education order challenged first to control and then slow down its progress, so it could readjust and maintain its former control or take credit for unleashing a new and progressive development. This led to the intellectual explosion we call the Enlightenment in the Western (European) world. It is important to note that this was an upper-class movement that only indirectly affected the mass of humanity in these societies but did contribute to the eventual growth of the middle class.

People became more impatient to get new ideas, news, and connections. The newspaper and magazine were born to satisfy these desires. Its low production cost and publication speed offered a new potential audience. The sticking point is that they needed to know how to read. The older order of education institutions demanded reading for their students to be able to read at least biblical text; ingenious industrialists saw it also as an avenue to further readership and thus sales for their growing newspaper and magazine industries.

"The enemy of my enemy is my friend" (ancient proverb). Massive education reform in the United States in the 19th and 20th centuries is linked to this development. The child labor reform movement succeeded partly because the progressives convinced the industrialists that a better-educated workforce leads to a better, more productive labor source.

Looking through the lens of American History, news stories have always been used to try to influence segments of targeted populations. Whether we are talking about the Federalist Papers, Yellow Journalism, picture news, the evening news broadcast, or the tweets and Tic Toks of today, the goal is to interpret the world around us to benefit the persons behind the published words and images.

Our vision of the world and how we interpret it results from a complex mixture of our intelligence, experience, and what we perceive as facts. Today's "cheap" source of information platforms lies in most of our hands: our phones. The reality of this is similar to what happened in our past; being able to be discriminating and critical consumers of information is our best, and in some ways, the only path to individual and collective informed growth.

Parents: The Guardians of Dreams

Understanding a world that is different than your own is challenging to grasp. When a parent(s) consciously approaches their child's future with a sense or desire to have an outcome different or better than their circumstances, however, they define it; it is the most powerful first step to a parent partnership that schools can and should leverage. My parents worked supporting individuals who had access (read: education, socialization, and networks) to life choices that would provide a more robust quality of life. The significant difference in their life and ultimate opportunities lay in the fact they needed more of a formal education and the network that formed as a result.

Much like children of the middle and upper classes, they network with those who surround their lives and learn and share pathways to the world they are a part of and beyond. Supporting that goal meant planning and directing us toward that expectation of choices in education and fields of eventual careers. Meanwhile, my parents were interested in the world they now found themselves in, the USA, and the home they left, Ireland. Keeping up with the news of the USA and the world was critical to them. The network of support they relied on was fellow Irish immigrants in the areas where we lived. These networks served as cultural support and pathways of connections and learning of opportunities and how those before them accessed them. These groups served as the jumping-off point for how parents could lead their children to other options that were not open to them.

School reform over the last 65 + years, roughly since *Sputnik*, has been aimed at improving the academic outcomes of our nation's youth. Much innovation in our approach to curriculum and recognition of special education needs is detailed in the archives of education research. Yet, despite waves of concentrated efforts and legislative actions, our schools continue to have a frustrating core of students labeled as "underperformers." Many efforts to positively affect change in the last 40 years have run the gamont of demanding via legislation or professional shaming of schools to institute more exacting accountability measures and changes to the rigor of curriculum and back to loosening accountability measures and curriculum rigor. This dizzying process is partly due to the lag effects of these actions: declining or stagnating student progress, however, measured, and a very real teacher and administration shortage as fewer and fewer individuals are taking up the call to be educators.

Recognizing Our Situation and Doing Something

Public Schools are the result of where they are located, meaning they reflect the social pecking order of people who can afford to live in those locations. Poorer people live in areas that are under-resourced compared to the needs of their students and need the chance of parents being able to provide extra resources. In the more affluent areas, the aid and support they receive go to enhancing opportunities rather than paying for needed primary education support. In the end, the type and access to opportunities for education far exceed those of the poorer students. Parent partnerships with their schools leveraging parents in their primary teacher role is the most direct and effective way to increase the opportunities and dreams of our most economically disadvantaged students.

Six versus 18 hours of influence: those who are not your family versus those who are a part of your flesh and blood. Supporting and encouraging curiosity and dreaming are the keys to creativity and the path to new and better realities.

If schools are alone in these approaches, they will wither on the vine if it's not nourished and valued at home. Schools are in the business of education and educating parents, and their tremendous influence is the more efficient approach to affecting choices and opportunities for our children.

Equity Is Not a Destination—The Longer View

Education is a process, and so is the state of equity. Equity of education has the means to seize opportunities available to everyone. As opportunities develop and grow, so must the education to take advantage of those dreams and the equity processes to ensure a meritocratic society. The promise of free and public education was founded on creating opportunity and a better-prepared society, not just for those families who could afford it. Progressive educators sold the industrialist and rugged individualist in the 19th century and the dawn of the 20th century that a better-educated workforce ensured a better society. The real quandary lies in the acceptance of actual competition for opportunities. Many claim that jobs simply being filled by persons in our society are the measurement of attaining opportunities; this could not be further from the truth. Quantifying what type of lifestyle quality these jobs can provide is necessary for a person to reach the point of education. To value education and the opportunities, it can lead to is to understand the lifestyle and quality of life it can support or be supported by that attainment. Otherwise, we develop a system in which we create a subsistence subculture that supports those born into an advantage at the expense of those who are not. To buy their acceptance, we point to things they can consume that we determine is their prize. We convince those disadvantaged (read: white) that their plight is because of others (read: black, brown, Asian) holding them back. This is absurd because many of these (white) people are also just as poor and ill-prepared for seizing education opportunities but are held at bay via our human need to rationalize our plight. Maslow argued that these individuals are stuck well below self-actualization and cannot accept the responsibility of choices. The point is that it is time to stop treating the lag indicators (attendance, discipline, college, and so on), but to recognize our efforts must turn to the lead indicators. Parents are the primary teachers; we put band aids on severed limbs without their efforts, abilities, and resources.

Giving Someone Stuff Doesn't Mean They Have a Clue How to Use It

Building it and they will come may be the formula for baseball fields, but it is not so for education. I can't accurately tell you how many unused computers were bought and just gained dust in schools across America during the mid-1980s into the early 2000s, but it was pretty significant. If I could collect a dollar from everyone who told me in some fashion that they "didn't do computers," I swear I could be a billionaire. Fast forward to March 2020, when our state shut down schools and immediately had them convert to "remote" learning. I witnessed teachers taking pictures of textbooks, sending those pages to students via email or on their class sites, and then having the students write something they would not get back for over a week. I even heard a computer visual arts teacher complaining about his difficulty with the Google Classroom platform and getting his students to engage.

I was honored to attend a virtual meeting to discuss our state's digital divide. It is a beautiful start, and what became apparent to me was the need to separate access to the internet (adding the big problem of the personal cost of maintaining internet service) and devices from the professional development/learning that is needed for teachers, parents, and students to transform education as we know it.

Before people get lost in the weeds of various programs, apps, and platforms, they first understand what digital technology is designed to accomplish and understand how good teaching practice may be enhanced (not replaced) by its use.

Once that need is understood, a systematic approach to support and education can be effectively created and collaboratively distributed.

Educate, It Is What We Do Best

Case Study: My Dad's Doctor Visit

I remember clearly how mad I got at my parents after they came back home after visiting the doctor. I asked them, "so what did the doctor say about the pain you were telling me about?" My dad was why they went to the office: "Ah, nothing, he didn't say anything." Me: "Really, he said nothing at all about your pain?" Dad: "He was useless." Me: "Did you tell him what has been going on and explain where and when the pain started and how long it has been going on?" Dad: "Why that is what he was there to tell me!" At that point, I ended the conversation. I should have understood where my parents were coming from, but I did not. My parents were intimidated by doctors and viewed them as people you go to only when you are sick, injured, or dying. They are expensive visits, and they felt overwhelmed and embarrassed that they did not keep up with regular checkups and feared that when they did go, the doctor would just sit in judgment of them. They did respect them but were conflicted about how they felt. This is not unlike how many of our less advantaged families feel when confronting schools and the education of their students.

As public educators, we serve the students, not the parents. They are our sole focus, so we need to ensure their best possible outcomes. The best outcomes can only happen when the students are supported in their education by their primary teachers during that 18-hour balance. The only way to help ensure that beyond happenchance is to assist and provide education and support to the parents. It takes the parent to raise the student; it takes the school and community to ensure the parents have what they need to accomplish this vital task. Educating is what we do best. Educating parents in their primary teaching role is the only way to move that 6 and 18 balance in favor of education equity.

College and Career Ready

Reading the headlines over the last few years, just before COVID-19 and since, about how we do not need to be "college and career ready, it all about career ready," or that "if the cost of going to college is more than what a student can earn in the profession, is it a worthwhile investment?" or the more basic, "is college a worthwhile investment?" Certainly, these are essential questions and considerations, but let us look at the "why" this is being asked. There is no doubt about the high cost of attending college, which is supported by just looking at reported tuition costs, problems with an increasing number of students defaulting on student loan debt, or others dropping out due to inability to afford the opportunity. Our national, state, regional, and local governments do not value the opportunity to make it more affordable at the expense of other budgetary choices. Our society feels that it is not as important as the day-to-day necessities, and those who can afford to pay a fair share of the burden do not want to give up the privilege of what they have without returning a value to themselves directly.

It is a fact that high school graduates make more money than high school dropouts, and college graduates make more than high school graduates. Burdens such as the cost of going to school make it impossible for the de facto segregation to stop in many cases. Our society attempts to "level" the playing field by concentrating on the poor to give them a financial step up. Still, even this is misguided—these people are least likely to take advantage. So much of the money set aside is not spent. Those fortunate enough to take advantage of the aid must contend with resentment of those who do not qualify for the aid but are not rich enough to pay to go fully. These people painfully see the advantage of going to college and supporting the pathway but cannot find a way to pay for it. Our poorest in society have more money available to them but do not have the vision, tools, and support to make it a reality. This is an equity quagmire.

In the 19th century, the push for free public high school only gained momentum when the progressives and industrialists saw the advantage of a better-educated working class. Also, at the same time, new professions emerged that looked to advance learning and preparation, which found their way to colleges and universities to validate the pursuits and valuation of emerging professions. These new studies required students to see the value of free public high schools in preparing more students for college studies. The GI Bill effect enormously built up our middle professional class during the post-WWII generation. Grateful for the sacrifice of so many and the need to fill ranks in our industry, vast amounts of money were made available to train and educate our veterans for our society during the Cold War period. Again, from multiple perspectives, our society saw a need and agreed on the process.

What is the calculus today? Is it cheaper to keep things where they are currently, a de facto pecking order of who can access all opportunities, and to keep a large group happy buying them with a few dollars of benefits while not affecting the structure? The luxury of immediate security versus future opportunity is available to those with means for others; it is not a choice. Is it cheaper to invest in our parent-teachers and help foster a new generation of students who have more choices in life or continue the struggle and strife in a society with layers of inequity based on color and socio-economic failure? Think rural inequity? These are hard choices, but they are not much more expensive in the long run than what is happening now.

Reflection

1 What were the most significant issues during the shutdown? Classify these: lack of knowledge, lack of stuff, and lack of access.
2 Write out what changes you wish to make at your school. Pick one of those changes, deep dive into what you need to make it happen, and update it constantly.

Resources
Typical Community Agencies

- State social service agencies: https://www.usa.gov/state-social-services (Retrieved January 3, 2024)
- Medicare.gov:https://www.medicare.gov/care-compare/ (Retrieved January 3, 2024)

Additional Resources

Darfler-Sweeney, P. (2018). *The superintendent's rulebook: A guide to district-level leadership.* Routledge: Abingdon, Oxfordshire, UK.

Dewey, J. (2023). Democracy and education: An introduction to the philosophy of education. Macmillan. New York.